Oscar Israelowitz

Guide
to
Jewish
EUROPE

Western Europe - 8th Edition

Israelowitz Publishing

P.O.Box 228 Brooklyn, New York 11229 Tel. (718) 951-7072

Copyright © 1993 by Oscar Israelowitz

All rights reserved. Reproduction in whole or part without permission is prohibited.

Library of Congress Catalogue Card Number: 84-090694
International Standard Book Number: 1-878741-05-5

Printed in the United States of America.

CONTENTS

Travel Tips

There have been problems in recent years concerning security around synagogues and Jewish community centers. There are now armed security guards and patrols standing near all of these institutions in the major cities throughout Europe. Be prepared to undergo security checks before entering any of these buildings. If you are Orthodox and do not carry your passport on the Sabbath, go to the synagogue before the onset of Sabbath with your passport and make the necessary arrangements with the security guards.

After synagogue services it is recommended to clear-away from the proximity of the synagogue or temple. Terrorists have attacked congregations in Rome as they were leaving synagogue services. In England and France, the rabbis warn people not to "hang-around" in front of the synagogue after services. Take heed.

Most breads in Europe are not kosher! The pans and trays in which breads are baked are usually smeared with lard or shortening. Hearth-baked breads are okay, if you can verify that they were not prepared with shortening.

It is recommended to purchase a box of matzohs in a kosher grocery. This will stay fresh and will keep you going until you reach a kosher restaurant or bakery.

Most breads in France are kosher. When buying bread in a bakery (only) be sure to ask if the bread is bakes *sans moulé*. It is recommended to ask the local rabbi if you have any doubts about breads. Most breads prepared with a glazed surface are not kosher.

The milk in Spain is not kosher! The heavy cream is removed and is replaced with (animal) fat. There is no government control over milk additives.

Some vinegars in Italy are made with (non-kosher) wine.

In Italy, there have been questions about the kashrut of meats. If you have any questions, ask the local rabbi in the city. The majority of meats are ritually slaughtered by the local rabbi or *shochet*. Some Ashkenazic people will not eat meats which were slaughtered by Sephardic shochtim.

Many European cities have trolley systems which do not have conductors aboard. These trolley systems (Zurich or Amsterdam) are designed on an honor system. You are required to purchased a ticket before you enter the tram at a machine on the tram station or at the main railroad terminal. If you are caught by an inspector, who might just happen to board your tram car, you will be given a stiff fine if you don't have a ticket, usually about $25, which must be paid on the spot. The Eurailpass is not valid on inner city trolleys or subways. In Zurich, it is best to buy the most expensive ticket (blue) which entitles the rider to unlimited tram rides for one day.

While visiting Holland, beware of the bicyclists! Most of the population uses bicycles as its primary means of transportation. They are fast and quiet. If you are crossing the street, they will shoot out of nowhere, and you can't even hear them coming. They are extremely dangerous to those who are in their way. So watch out for the bikes!

Before boarding an intercity train in Spain it is necessary to make a reservation for your seat. Even if you hold a Eurailpass, this reservation is required due to the very limited seats on the trains.

There are no baggage-storage areas in Spanish train terminals. This is due to the precaution against terrorist bombings. Some stores near the train terminals will watch your bags, for a fee.

In England, when crossing the street, always look to the right! Traffic patterns are reversed in England, although the British say that everyone else is reversed.

In the London Underground (subway or metro), always hold onto your ticket, since you must show it to a guard before leaving the exit.
There is a "Day-Pass" available (for about two pounds), which entitles the holder to unlimited underground and bus travel throughout London (non-rush hours only). It's a real bargain.

When taking intercity trains, be sure to check the destination markers on the outside of each train car. Sometimes, long trains are broken into segments; each going to a different destination.

Note: All timetables in this guide are in *military time.*

AUSTRIA

The first record of Jewish presence in Austria dates back to 906. There was a Jewish colony in Judenburg, one of the oldest towns in Austria. Vienna's first synagogue was established in 1204. A ghetto was established in the 13th century around the square called *Judenplatz*.

Vienna was recognized as the leading community of German Jewry. Among the "Sages of Vienna" were the rabbis Isaac Or Sarua, Avigdor ben Eliyahu ha-Cohen, and Meir ben Baruch ha-Levi.

Duke Albert V's need for money combined with the hatred for the Jews among the Christians led to the cruel persecutions in 1421 (the Viener Geserah). The Jews were driven from the city. The Vienna Synagogue was razed, its stones being used in the construction of the new building of the University of Vienna; all Jewish property was expropriated; and many Jews were burned at the stake.

The second Jewish community was established in 1624. Jews were permitted to live on the estates of the aristocracy but had to pay an exorbitant tax. The community was enlarged following the Chmielnicki pogroms in Poland in 1648. The Jewish community in Vienna was centered on the site of today's

Leopoldstadt. There were 500 families. Its notable scholars included rabbis Yom Tov Lipman Heller and Shabbetai Sheftal Horovitz.

This period of tolerance did not last long. In 1670, anti-Jewish feelings among the Christians and the religious fanatacism of the emperor's wife, prompted Emperor Leopold I's decision to expel the Jews from Vienna, to sell their homes, and to convert the main synagogue into a church.

This expulsion proved so economically disastrous that some Jews were invited to return as Court bankers and imperial war purveyors. These "Court Jews" included such notables as Samuel Oppenheimer, Samson Wertheimer (named Chief Rabbi of Hungary in 1693), and Diego Aguilar, the founder of Vienna's Sephardic community.

Vienna became the center for Hebrew publishing and, in the early 19th century, was the center of the Haskalah (Enlightenment) Movement. The magnificent Stadttempel was built in 1826. It was the result of a compromise reached by the Reform and the traditional Jews in the city.

Jews participated in the Revolution of 1848 and were granted equal rights in 1867. A "Golden Age" for the Jews followed. Theodor Herzl lived and worked in

Vienna. Vienna became the center of Zionism.

Following World War I, the Austro-Hungarian Empire was dismantled. The situation for the Jews began to disintegrate. In 1938, there were 180,000 Jews in Vienna. This population was virtually wiped out. There are about 8,000 permanent Jewish residents. There are an additional 4,000 Jews-in-transit. They are recent Russian refugees either coming out of the Soviet Union or are "drop-outs" from Israel. There are also many Iranian Jewish refugees living in Vienna.

Eisenstadt

GHETTO SITE   Judengasse

Located near the castle of Prince Esterhazy, the ghetto was established in the mid-sixteenth century. The Jews maintained an autonomous community with its own police and fire departments, judges and mayor. This community was totally destroyed by the Nazis in 1938.

JEWISH MUSEUM   Museumgasse & Unterberggasse

This museum was founded in 1902 by a local wealthy wine merchant, Sandor Wolf. It is now part of the County Museum.

JEWISH CEMETERY   Wertheimgasse

This ancient cemetery dates from the 17th century.

WERTHEIMER SYNAGOGUE

This synagogue was built in 1750 by Samson Wertheimer, the Vienna Court Jew. It has recently been restored and designated a national landmark.

Judenburg

POST HOTEL   Hauptplace (Town Square)

The Post Hotel is said to have been a synagogue before the Jews were expelled in 1496. There is a carved figure of a bearded Jew's head wearing a peaked hat, on the south façade.

Mauthausen

CONCENTRATION CAMP

Located about 30 miles from Linz, the former concentration camp is now maintained as a national monument. The original torture cells, gas chamber, and crematoria have been left intact.

Vienna

FREUD'S HOUSE   19 Berggasse

The second-floor apartment where Dr. Sigmund Freud lived and worked from 1891 to 1938 has been preserved as a museum. Only the intervention of President Roosevelt enabled the Freuds to escape to England, after payment of a huge ransom. Freud died in London in 1939.

JEWISH CEMETERIES 9 Seegasse

This site was the center of the medieval Jewish community. It is the oldest surviving Jewish burial site in Austria. The oldest tombstone dates from 1450. Samson Oppenheimer, the Court Jew who founded the third Jewish community in Vienna, is buried here. This cemetery was closed in 1783.

The present Jewish cemetery is located at 11 Simmeringer Hauptstrasse. The "Who's Who" of Vienna's Jewry are buried in this cemetery, including the Rothschilds and Ignas Brull, the teacher of Gustav Mahler.

STADTEMPLE (CITY TEMPLE) & JEWISH MUSEUM
4 Seittenstettengasse   Tel. 36-16-55 (14)

The first synagogue on this site was built in 1811. It was dismantled in 1817 and replaced with a larger structure in 1826. The Stadttempel was designed by Josef Kornhausel. The authorities refused to let non-Catholic religious buildings be visible to the public, and thus the synagogue is wedged between two five-storey apartment houses which conceal it from the street. The front façade of the synagogue building looks similar to the adjoining apartment buildings. This anti-Semitic restriction spared this synagogue from being destroyed by the Nazis. The Nazis, however, did totally destroy all of Vienna's other synagogues in 1938. There were over sixty synagogues in Vienna before the war.

The construction of the synagogue had been delayed by controversies between the Reform and Conservative parties in the congregation. One of the debates was whether or not to have an organ. The synagogue was dedicated on April 9, 1826, to the accompaniment of music by the Christian composer, Jacob Drechsler, who was the choir master at St. Stephan's Cathedral. The cantor, Solomon Sulzer, and the Reform-minded rabbi, Isak Noah Manheimer, had asked other eminent composers, including Beethoven, to compose music for that occasion. The cantor did obtain, at a later date, a setting for Psalm 92 from Schubert.

The gracious synagogue was designed behind a residential façade. It has an oval floor plan, an elliptical dome, and a narrow two-tiered gallery carried by a twelve-bay giant Ionic colonnade. The synagogue has recently been restored. The adjoining buildings house a number of small prayer rooms as well as several Jewish communal institutions. There is a kosher restaurant (Noah's Ark) next to the synagogue at Seittenstettengasse 2.

Note: This synagogue has been attacked by terrorists several years ago. There are armed patrols in front of the synagogue. Be prepared to show your passport if you wish to enter the synagogue complex.

SIMON WIESENTHAL DOCUMENTATION CENTER

Salztorgasse 6

This center is noted for hunting Nazi war criminals. If you wish to visit, it is necessary to make an appointment by calling 63-91-31.

KOSHER PROVISIONS

Bad Gastein   Hotel Erzherzog Johan   *Tel. 2690*

Semmering

Pension Alexander   *Hochstraase 87   Tel. 026-64-336*

Vienna

 Arche Noah (restaurant)

  Seitenstettengasse 2/Judengasse   Tel. 533-13-74

Englander   (bakery) *Hollandstrasse 3   Tel. 33-42-46*

Rebenwurzel   (butcher) *Singerstrasse 24   Tel.   512-13-20*

Resetritsch   (grocery) *Grosse Pfarrgasse 6   Tel. 33-42-46*

Tuv Taam   *Franzhochedlinger Gasse 23*

(groceries)   *Hollandstraase 10   Tel. 26-96-75*

    Tempelgasse 8   Tel. 24-83-94

Jewish Welcome Service (Vienna)

Stephansplatz 10   Tel. 63-88-91

SYNAGOGUES

Graz *Grieskai 58   Tel. 912-468*

Innsbruck   *Zollerstrasse 1   Tel. 26892*

Linz   *Bethlehemstrasse 26   Tel. 279-805*

Salzburg   *Mertensstrasse 7   Tel. 5665*

Vienna

Stadttempel *Seitenstettengasse 4   Tel. 36-16-55*

Agudas Yisroel   *Grunangergasse 1   Tel.   512-83-31*

    Tempelgasse 3   Tel. 24-92-62

Ohel Moshe   *Lilienbrunngasse 19   Tel. 26-88-64*

Machsike Haddas   *Fleischmark 1   Tel. 26-14-813*

Misrachi   *Judenplatz 8   Tel. 535-41-53*

Agudas Yeshurun   *Riemergasse 9*
Schiffschul   *Grosse Schiffgasse 8*
Shomre Haddas   *Glasergasse 17*
Sephardic Cong.   *Praterstrasse 23   Tel. 24-69-022*
Chabad-Lubavitch   *Grunentorgasse 26   Tel. 31-11-49*

MIKVEHS

Salzburg   *Lasserstrasse 8   Tel. 5665*
Vienna
Tempelgasse 3   Tel. 24-92-62
Fleischmarkt 22   Tel. 52-52-62
Lilienbrunngase 19   Tel. 26-88-44

RAILROAD TIMETABLE

Vienna to: Amsterdam.................. 7.20 - 20.54
Berlin............................ 9.30 - 22.12
Copenhagen................ 7.20 - 6.45
London.......................... 20.50 - 18.58
Paris.............................. 8.00 - 23.15
Rome............................. 7.55 - 23.50
Stockholm..................... 7.20 - 9.00 (next day)
Venice........................... 7.55 - 16.54
Zurich............................ 7.00 - 16.28

BELGIUM

There were Jewish settlements throughout Belgium in the 14th century. Jews were accused of well poisoning and witchcraft during the Bubonic Plague of 1348. Five hundred Jews in Brussels were slaughtered in 1370 after being accused of desecrating a Christian religious symbol. There are still streets called *Rue de Juifs* and *Jodenstraat* (Jews Street) in Antwerp, Ghent, Mons, Eupen, Tienen, and Wasmes. These are reminders of former Jewish settlements in the Middle Ages.

Marrano (secret) Jews who fled from Spain after the Inquisition in 1492, found refuge in Belgium. The Rodriguez family, of noted Marrano descent, introduced the diamond industry to Belgium. That industry has developed Antwerp into one of the world's major diamond centers.

The Jews were given complete religious equality in 1794. In the 1880s, many Eastern European Jews moved to Belgium. Today's Jewish community is descended from this last group of immigrants. During World War II, many Jews fled to England, Switzerland, and Cuba. Many Christians hid Jews in their homes during this period. There was a major network of Belgian Christians who were involved in rescuing

Jewish children from deportation. Nevertheless, 26,000 Belgian Jews were deported to the concentration camps.

There are today approximately 41,000 Jews in Belgium. The main Jewish centers are located in Antwerp and Brussels.

Antwerp

The closely-knit Jewish community of Antwerp is composed primarily of Orthodox Jews. They live and work near the central railroad terminal. As the trains approach the central terminal, there are large synagogues visible on either side of the tracks. Most of the community is involved in the diamond trade. There are several kosher restaurants, bakeries, and butchers all within walking distance from the central station. There is even an *eruv* in Antwerp. During the past decade, there have been several terrorist attacks against Jewish houses of worship and businesses. There are now many armed security patrols throughout the city.

BOUWMEESTERSTRAAT SYNAGOGUE

This synagogue is the oldest Jewish house of worship in the city. It was designed in 1893 by a Christian architect, Ernest Stordian. Its style is Moorish Revival.

ROMI GOLDMUNTZ CENTER

Nervierstraat 12   Tel. 239-39-11

This is where you will meet the local Jewish community

members. The center offers concerts, lecture programs, game rooms, and socials. You will hear all of the different languages spoken by the Jews of Antwerp, including Flemish, Hebrew, Yiddish, French, and English.

DIAMOND BOURSE   Pelikaanstraat

The Diamond Bourse (Club) is off-limits to non-members. There are hundreds of armed security guards and electronic surveillance devices throughout this district. You must be "invited-in" by a member of the Bourse.

There is a way of seeing how diamonds are cut, polished, etc. A facsimile of the Bourse has been set up. It is called *Diamondland,*. It is located at Appelmansstraat 33A. Admission is free but passports must be shown. For further information call 234-36-12.

SEPHARDIC SYNAGOGUE   Hovenierstraat 31

Built in 1913 by a Jewish architect, Joseph DeLange. It was designed in Romanesque-Byzantine eclectic. This synagogue is located in the heart of the Diamond Center. It was attacked by terrorists in 1982. Photographs are not permitted even outside of the synagogue due to security reasons.

Brussels

GREAT SYNAGOGUE   Rue de la Regence

(Enter at 2 Rue Dupont)   Tel. 512-21-90

This synagogue was built in 1878 in Romanesque Revival style by a Christian architect, Desire DeKeyser. The Belgian Jewish Museum is housed in this building. The ancient medieval ghetto site, at Rue Ravenstein, was located several blocks north of this synagogue.

There is a new synagogue located in the suburbs of Brussels which was designed to resemble a 17th century wooden synagogue of Poland. All of the windows, however, are filled with bullet-proof glass - a sign of the times. It is located at Avenue Messidor 11 and is called the Synagogue Maale.

Side Trips

During the summer vacation, the Belgian Jews flock to the seaside resort community in Knokke. There is a kosher grocery in that town, only during the summer season.

A very worthwhile side trip should be made to the medieval City of Bruges. It has picturesque canals and has been called the "Venice of the North."

If you are in Brussels, be sure to visit the Grand' Place in the heart of the city. Also, be sure to take a ride on the new subway (metro) out to the 1958 World's Fair site. The subway was designed by several architectural and graphic design firms. There are murals painted along the station walls. Musak is piped into each station. There are statues of the Belgian royal family, dressed in 16th century attire, assembled along the station walls. Some stations have precast concrete columns which are textured to appear as if they are tree trunks. There are also pastoral landscape scenes painted on some station walls. In short, it's a fun trip.

KOSHER PROVISIONS

Antwerp

Blue Lagoon   *Appelmanstr. 18   Tel.   226-01-14*

Hoffy's Take Away Restaurant

Lange Lievietstraat 52   Tel.   234-35-35

Gelkop   *Van Leriusstraat 28   Tel.   233-07-53*

Dresdner   *Simonstraat 10   Tel.   232-60-42*

Kleinblatt Bakery   *Provincierstraat & Wippstraat*

Brussels

Chez Gilles   (restaurant)   *52 rue Gheide   Tel. 523-94-22*

Yarkow   (mini market)

85 Avenue des Sept Bonniers   Tel.   344-17-29

(bakery)   *62 rue de Suede   (St. Gilles)   Tel.   537-16-79*

Lanxner   *(butcher)*

121 rue de Brabant   (Shaerbeek)   Tel.   217-26-20

(butcher)   *37 avenue Jean Volders   Tel.   537-06-08*

Knokke   Steinmentz   *Kongostraat 1   Tel. 61-02-65*

SYNAGOGUES

Antwerp

ISRAELITISCHE GEMEENTE

Terlistraat 35   Tel.   235-41-47

Bouwmeestersstraat

Isabellalei 65

Vanden Nestei

Hovenierstraat 31

ISRAELITISCHE ORTHODOXE GEMEENTE

Beth Hamedrash Hagadol   *Oostenstraat 43   Tel.   230-92-46 van Leriusstraat 54*

Belzer   *van Spangenstraat 6   Tel.   231-94-48*

Bobover   *Lg. Leemstr. 222   Tel.   239-71-05*

Gerer   *Antoon van Dykstraat 43   Tel.   239-72-74*

Lubavitcher   *Plantijn Moretuslei 49*

Satmar   *Jacob Jacobstraat 6*

Vishnitzer   *Brialmontlei 16*

Sanzer *van Leriusstraat 37   Tel.   232-90-97*

Oonsciencestraat 40

Eisenmann Shul   *Oostenstraat 29*

Marsstraat 40

van Leriusstraat 22

Beth Yitzchak   *Mercatorstraat 56*

Brussels

Ahavat Re'im   *73 rue de Thy   Tel. 648-38-37*

Beth Hamedrash   *rue de Chapeau   Tel. 521-12-89*

Synagogue Maale   *Avenue Messidor 11   Tel. 345-92-10*

Beth Israel   *101 avenue Stalingrad*

Beth Israel   *3 rue Houzeau de Lehaye*

Great Synagogue   *32 rue de la Regence*

Machzikei Hadas   *67A rue de la Clinique*

 Adath Israel *126 rue Rogier   Tel.   241-16-64*

Sephardic   *47 rue du Pavillon   Tel. 215-21-38*

Lubavitcher   (Rabbi Chaikin)

        1A avenue Reine Marie Henritte   Tel.   87-867

LIBERAL

96 avenue Kersbeek   Tel. 345-59-92

Charleroi   *56 rue Pige- au Croly*

Ghent   *14 Savaenstraat*

Knokke

Synagogue Van Bunnenlaan 30   Tel.   (050) 61-03-72

Liege   *19 rue L. Frederic*

Mons   *49 Grand Rue*

Ostend   *10 Maastrichtplein*

MIKVEHS

Antwerp

Steebokstraat 22   Tel.   239-75-88

van Diepenbeecksstraat 42   Tel. 239-09-65

Brussels

67A rue de la Clinique   Tel. 521-12-89

RAILROAD TIMETABLE

Brussels to: Amsterdam .... 9.10 - 12. 07

Berlin .... 9.48 - 20.40

Copenhagen .... 6.48 - 19.45

London .... 9.59 - 14.31

Paris .... 10.10 - 13.00

Rome .... 18.02 - 13.45

Vienna .... 7.48 - 21.28

Zurich ....12.12 - 19.57

DENMARK

Denmark was the first of the Scandinavian countries to allow Jewish settlement. The earliest arrivals, in 1622, was a small group of Sephardic Jews from Amsterdam and Hamburg. They were granted full religious freedom and commercial privileges. Other Sephardic Jews followed, serving as financiers and jewelers to the royal family and the Danish nobility. The Talmudic scholar, Benjamin Musafia, was named King Christian IV's personal physician in 1646. His son-in-law, Gabriel Milan, was appointed governor of the Danish West Indies (now th Virgin Islands) in 1684.

Danish hospitality to successive waves of Jewish immigrants has always been one of the country's proud traditions. The so-called "Viking Jews" - those who settled before 1903 - were followed in that year by the Russian Jews fleeing the Kishinev pogroms. Other refugees from Eastern Europe came after World War I and from Nazi Germany during the 1930s.

The Nazis had planned a round-up of Denmark's 8,000 Jews on October 1, 1943, the second day of Rosh Hashanah, when every Jew would be conveniently assembled in the synagogue or at home, easy prey for the special Kommando units of the Gestapo, which were hand-picked by Adolf Eichmann himself for their mission. German troopships were anchored in Copenhagen Harbor, ready to transport all the Jews to the death camps of central Europe.

But when the stormtroopers, in a series of carefully executed, simultaneous raids, descended upon the Great Synagogue and upon the Jewish homes, they found that their prey had vanished. Virtually every Jewish man, woman and child in the country had been hidden away in the homes of fellow-Danes, in basements and attics, in churches and hospitals. During the ten days that followed, between Rosh Hashanah and Yom Kippur, the Jews were smuggled out of the country and taken by an improvised fleet of fishing vessels and row boats, to safe haven in Sweden. Their escape route was via Elsinore (the site of Shakespeare's "Hamlet") and across the narrow waters of Oresund. Today, there are about 7,500 Jews in Denmark.

Copenhagen

GREAT SYNAGOGUE   12 Krystalglade

Influenced by the scientific expedition attached to Napoleon's armies in Egypt, the architect Gustav Friedrich Hetsch of Stuttgart, designed the Great Synagogue of Copenhagen in 1833 with elements of Egyptian and Greek architecture. Its plain exterior does not prepare the visitor for the white-and-gold elegance of the interior. Services are conducted daily, on the Sabbath, and Jewish Festivals by Denmark's Chief Rabbi. There is a special *kiddush* for visitors on Friday evenings.

JEWISH COMMUNITY CENTER

6 Ny Kongensgade   Tel. 0193 0668

The Jewish Community Center contains a kosher cafeteria, a small museum, library and a mikveh.

ROUND TOWER   Kobmagergade

Adjoining Trinity Church, within site of the Great Synagogue, the Round Tower was where the sacred Torahs of the Jewish community were hidden during the Nazi occupation.

HOLMEN'S CHURCH BELFRY

The Holmens Canal was the first station in the Danish Jews' underground escape-route to Sweden in 1943.

ROYAL DANISH LIBRARY   8 Christians Brygge

This library houses one of the largest Jewish book collections in the world. Known as the Bibliotheca Judaica Simonseniana, it contains maore than 50,000 volumes of Hebraica and Judaica, and hundreds of precious manuscripts, some dating from the 13th and 14th centuries.

MUSEUM OF THE DANISH RESISTANCE

Esplanaden

This museum is devoted to the history and exploits of the Danish Resistance during World War II. The museum also features an exhibit of maps and photographs depicting the rescue of the Danish Jews from Hitler, their escape-route, their reception in Sweden and the welcome accorded them on their return to Denmark in 1945.

ISRAELSPADS (ISRAEL SQUARE)

Located in the center of the city, this square was formerly known as "Green Square," since it had been for 200 years, the site of an open-air vegetable market. It was re-named Israel Square in 1968, on the 25th anniversary of the rescue of Danish Jews during the war. Its counterpart in Jerusalem is called "Denmark Square," a token of Israel's "Thanks to Scandinavia."

JEWISH CEMETERY

One of the oldest Jewish cemeteries in northern Europe is located on the Moellegade. The earliest of its 5,500 well-preserved tombstones marks the grave of David Israel, an early Jewish settler from Hamburg, Germany, who died in Denmark in 1693.

KOSHER PROVISIONS

Copenhagen

Community Center Cafeteria   *6 Ny Kongensgade*

Tel. 0193 0668

Kosher Caterers: *Rorholmdgade   Tel. 13 30 12*

Classengade 5   Tel. 42 09 81

Vendersgade 16   Tel. 11 70 63

SYNAGOGUES

Copenhagen

Great Synagogue *12 Krystalgade*

Hornbaek Synagogue *Granvej 7   Tel. 20 07 31*

Machzike Hadass *12 Ole Suhrsgade   Tel. 12 77 99*

MIKVEH

Copenhagen

6 Ny Kongensgade   Tel. 0193 0668

RAILROAD TIMETABLE

Copenhagen to:

Amsterdam	10.10 - 21.32
Berlin	10.12 - 20.35
Frankfurt	7.20 - 17.31
Helsinki	8.19 - 9.00 (next day)
London	9.25 - 9.14
Milan	7.20 - 5.25
Oslo	9.34 - 19.31
Paris	8.19 - 16.47
Vienna	13.10 - 9.50

ENGLAND

Jewish settlement in England was encouraged by William the Conqueror during his reign (1066-1089). The Jews were permitted only to be moneylenders. They did not live in ghettos but rather congregated in certain streets - one of which was generally called "Jewry" - close to a place of royal protection. Next to the king, Aaron the Jew from Lincoln, was the wealthiest Jew of his day in England. He was head of a chain of moneylending offices and provided the funds that built the great cathedrals of Lincoln and Peterborough.

During the first two centuries of Jewish settlement in England, there had been periods of reasonable security. The Jews were free to travel and enjoyed a large measure of communal autonomy. Starting in the 12th century, however, there were accusations of ritual murders, persecutions, and even massacres of Jews. This culminated with the edict of Edward I, dated July 18, 1290, which expelled all Jews from England. The decree took effect on All Saints' Day of 1290. Some three thousand Jews were driven from British soil, and would not return officially for over 365 years.

The Inquisition in Spain and Portugal, in the end of

the 15th century, created the Marrano - a secret Jew, who practiced Catholicism in public but practiced Judaism in private. Many Marranos came to England during the 15th and 16th centuries, but did not reveal their true identity until 1656, when Oliver Cromwell permitted Jews to officially resettle in England.

Cromwell was influenced by Menasseh ben Israel, the Chief Rabbi of Amsterdam, who was a Marrano by birth. Menasseh ben Israel's petition stated that the Messiah will not come until the Jews were to be scattered over the four corners of the earth. The Puritans of England believed in the advent of the Messiah and therefore re-admitted the Jews. Cromwell was appreciative of what Jewish merchants could do for English trade.

In 1657, the Spanish and Portuguese Jews organized the first Jewish house of worship in England. The second congregation was established by Ashkenazic Jews from Germany in 1690. These early settlers contributed many distinguished figures, represented by such great families as the Rothschilds, Montefiores, Sassoons, and Goldsmids.

The most important change within the life of Anglo-Jewry came with the period of mass immigration from Eastern Europe, in the years between 1881 and 1914.

Starting with the assassination of Czar Alexander II in 1881, a massive wave of terror in the form of pogroms, brought over 235,000 Jews to England.

The newcomers provided a complete contrast to the assimilated older Jewish community, in which they were at first, not altogether welcome. Their habits and their dress were different, and they knew no English. They were a distinct element, overcrowding the East End of London, and forming ghettos in the large provincial cities.

Old clothes dealing was the Jewish occupation. The old clothes markets were in Petticoat Lane, in the heart of London's Jewish quarter. Scenes of London's East End closely paralleled what was going on across the Atlantic Ocean, in New York City's Lower East Side, at the turn of the 20th century.

The old Jewish sections of England's major cities are presently inhabited by low-income groups: Indian, Pakistani, and blacks. The Jews, for the most part, have moved away from these neighborhoods and have settled in the suburbs. There are today about 330,000 Jews in England.

Brighton

HEBREW CONGREGATION

66 Middle Street   Tel. (0273) 27785

Built in 1874 by architect Thomas Laison, the Hebrew Congregation of Brighton was designed as a private synagogue for the family of Sir Albert Sassoon. Sassoon was a member of the noted family of industrialists, traders, statesmen, poets, and entrepreneurs. The synagogue is dominated by its exquisite brass furnishings. The Ark is enclosed by two brass gates, appearing as a gilded cage.

The Bombay Bar (St. George's Road & Paston Place) was the mausoleum of Sir Albert Sassoon and his son. The remains were removed in 1933.

Bury St. Edmunds

MOYSES HALL

Located on the Cornhill, the Moyses Hall is believed to have been an 11th century Jewish residence. Some say that it was originally built as a synagogue. It is one of the oldest surviving Norman buildings in England. During the massacres of 1190, the only Jews who survived found refuge in this building. Moyses Hall is now a museum.

Gateshead

This seaport town is the home of the world renowned Gateshead Yeshiva. The Yeshiva is located at 50 Berwick Road. The Kollel (rabbinical training college) is located at 22

Claremont Place. There is also a women's teachers' training college at 50 Berwick Road.

Lincoln

JEWS HOUSE & JEWS COURT   Steep Hill

These two structures were built in Norman style during the 12th century. They are said to be the oldest private stone dwellings in England. Jews Court is believed to have been the synagogue. There is still a niche along the eastern wall of the large assembly hall. That niche contained the Torah scrolls.

There are rumors that the Jews Court is haunted. The present-day caretaker attests that while he was working in the former synagogue, he felt a "friendly spirit" drift across the room (and all windows were shut). Jews Court is now a museum.

Jews House was said to belong to the wealthy Jewess named Bellaset. Both the Jews House and Jews Court are national monuments.

AARON'S HOUSE   Steep Hill

Further up the hill, on the corner, stands the old Norman structure built during the 12th century, known as Aaron's House. This was the home of Aaron the Jew, one of the wealthiest men in all of England. As head of a chain of moneylending offices, he provided the funds that built the cathedrals of Lincoln and Peterborough.

LINCOLN CATHEDRAL

This cathedral dominates the town of Lincoln. It is located on

Jews Court is believed to have been a 12th century synagogue.

top of the hill. Its construction was financed by Aaron the Jew. In 1255, an eight-year-old boy named Hugh was found murdered near the cathedral. The Jews were accused of murdering the child as part of a ritual (using the blood of the child to make matzohs). This incident touched off massacres of Jews in many British cities. The Jews were totally expelled from England in 1290.

The shrine of "Little St. Hugh" is located in the south aisle of the Lincoln Cathedral.

Liverpool

OLD HEBREW CONGREGATION

Princes Road   Tel. 051 709-3431

This congregation was founded in 1870 by Jewish emigrants from Germany and Austria who were headed for the United States. When they got to Liverpool they changed their minds and decided to stay and settle in this city. The magnificent Old Hebrew Congregation was built in 1874. It is presently located in the black section of the city.

London

Note: London Underground stations are in italics.

OLD JEWRY *Bank Station (Northern Line)*

This small street, just off Poultry Street, was once the heart of the pre-Expulsion Jewish community.

JEWRY *Aldgate Station (Circle Line)*

This was the center of the Jewish community in pre-Expulsion London, after they were forced to move from Old Jewry because of anti-Semitic riots, at the time of Richard I's coronation.

DUKE'S PLACE SYNAGOGUE SITE
Aldgate Station (Circle Line)

The Great Synagogue of London, the Duke's Place Shul, was the mother congregation of the German or Ashkenazic Jews and was organized in 1690. The synagogue which stood at this location was built in 1790 and was designed by architect James Spillar.

The Neoclassical building seated 750 people, and was *the* synagogue of British Jewry where all of the community's major celebrations took place. In May, 1941, the Great Synagogue was bombed by the Nazis during the Blitzkrieg over London. Today, all that remains of the Great Synagogue is an historic plaque. The congregation relocated to London's West End following the war. They are now housed in the Marble Arch Synagogue.

SITE OF FIRST SYNAGOGUE
- AFTER THE RESETTLEMENT Creechurch Lane
Aldgate Station (Circle Line)

The first Jewish house of worship after the Resettlement of the Jews in England was opened in 1657, in the upper floor of a house in Creechurch Lane, which is located at the corner of Bury Street, at the base of the Cunard Line Building. An historic plaque is located just around the corner from the Bevis Marks Synagogue.

BEVIS MARKS SYNAGOGUE   4 Heneage Lane
Aldgate Station (Circle Line)

The oldest in England, Congregation Shaar Hashamayim, the Spanish and Portuguese Synagogue, located in Bevis Marks, was organized in 1657. Its first location was at Creechurch Lane and Bury Street, just around the corner from the present site.

This Sephardic congregation modelled its synagogue after the Great Portuguese Synagogue of Amsterdam. It was designed in 1701 by master-builder, Joseph Avis. Mr. Avis, a Quaker,

Bevis Marks Synagogue was organized in 1657.

refused to accept the overpayment of the construction costs for this house of worship. It is said that Queen Anne presented an oak beam from one of the royal navy's ships. It was to be incorporated in the roof of the building.

The Bevis Marks Synagogue measures 80 by 50 feet. The magnificent wooden Ark, resembling a reredos, is built in the Classical architectural style, in the manner of Sir Christopher Wren's time. There are seven great hanging many-branched candalabra, which are still used to light the building with candlelight on Sabbaths, Festivals, and during wedding ceremonies. The seven represent the days of the week. There are ten brass candlesticks before the Ark, symbolizing the Ten Commandments. The twelve columns supporting the women's gallery represent the twelve tribes of Israel.

There are morning services in the Bevis Marks Synagogue only on Mondays, Thursdays, and Saturdays at 7:30 a.m.

Recently, the congregation was having financial difficulties. The Board of Directors of the congregation decided to sell a parcel of land in front of the historic synagogue building. Today, there is a four-story office building standing in front of the old courtyard of the Bevis Marks Synagogue. The pediment from the original 1701 limstone portal was removed from that structure and incorporated within the front façade of the new yellow brick office complex.

PETTICOAT LANE   *Aldgate Station (Circle Line)*

The East End of London was similar to New York City's Lower East Side around the turn of the 20th century. It was the first home for thousands of Jewish refugees, fleeing from the pogroms of Eastern Europe after 1881. Most were unskilled laborers, so they worked in the garment industries. Many peddled old clothing in the market in Petticoat Lane, which was the heart of London's Jewish quarter.

Sunday mornings are still active as the "street market." Some of the old Yiddish-speaking merchants have been replaced with the newer immigrants - from India and Pakistan. Wentworth Street is the weekday marketplace.

FORMER SYNAGOGUE   48a Artillery Lane

The building housing the "Cosmart House-Felas Farms," was originally built as a synagogue, around the turn of the 20th century. Notice the cupola above the roof.

SANDY'S ROW SHUL

At the corner of Artillery Lane and Sandy's Row stands one of the few remaining synagogues in London's East End. It was built in 1854 and there are still weekly Sabbath services.

SOUP KITCHEN FOR THE JEWISH POOR
Brune Street

In order to feed the masses of Jewish poor, following the major wave of immigration around the turn of the 20th century, the Jewish relief agencies set up soup kitchens. The one located on Brune Street was built in 1902. The engraved entablature reads, "Soup Kitchen for the Jewish Poor." There are still some elderly Jewish people living in this section. This soup kitchen is still in operation. It gives out many parcels of food to these elderly Jews, especially before the holiday of Passover.

FORMER SYNAGOGUE   19 Princelet Street

This was a tenement-style synagogue, similar to the ones found in New York City's Lower East Side during the same period. There are now plans on restoring this building by the Spitafields Trust. It will be turned into a Museum of Immigration.

FORMER MACHZIKEI HADASS SYNAGOGUE

59 Brick Lane (corner Fournier Street)

Built in 1763 as a Huguenot (French) church, the building, for many years, housed a Jewish congregation, Machzikei Hadass. It was recently purchased by the local Bengali groups and have turned the building into a mosque. Notice the entablature of the Ten Commandment tablets and the Latin inscription below, along the Fournier Street façade.

FORMER SYNAGOGUE   2b Heneage Street

Just east of Brick Lane stands a former synagogue. It is presently used as a food market, specializing in Indian and Pakistani foods. As you enter the store, the women's gallery is still identifiable.

SITE OF THE PUBLIC BATHS

Old Castle Street (near Whitechapel Street)

Many of the tenements which housed the poor Jewish immigrants, at the turn of the 20th century, did not have bathtubs or showers. The public baths were built to accommodate these poor immigrants.

SITE OF JEWS FREE SCHOOL   Aldgate Street

This school, sponsored by the Jewish relief agencies, was located near the Brune Street soup kitchens. The remains of the bombed-out building now house shops and warehouses. The Jews Free School was located between Frying Pan Alley, Bell Lane, and Middlesex Street.

FORMER SYNAGOGUES

There are several abandoned synagogues in the East End of London and in the vicinity of Whitechapel, Spitafields, Stepney Green, Mile End, and West Ham. These areas have been designated as Urban Renewal districts. Many of these old synagogue buildings may be demolished in the very near future. Below is a partial list of former synagogue sites:

Whitechapel Road & Old Castle Street

Alie Street & Leman Street

Old Montague Street & Mount Hope Street

Deal Street & Chicksand Street

Thrawl Street (Yeshiva Etz Chaim)

SITE OF THE JEWS' TEMPORARY SHELTER

63 Mansell Street

This was the place where thousands of newly-arrived Jewish immigrants from Eastern Europe found temporary shelter, between the years 1881 and 1914.

JEWISH CEMETERIES

Mile End Station (District Line)

The oldest Jewish cemetery (Beth Haim Velho) is situated

behind the former Sephardic Home for the Aged, at 253 Mile End Road. It is the first Resettlement cemetery and was acquired in 1657. Such personalities as Abraham Fernandez Carvajal, regarded as the founder of the modern Anglo-Jewish community, Haham David Nieto, a great Sephardic leader, and Dr. Fernando Mendes, the physician who attended Charles II at his deathbed, are buried here.

The second oldest Jewish cemetery is located at Alderny Road. It was opened in 1696 by the Ashkenazic organizers of the Duke's Place Synagogue.

The Beth Haim Novo is located at 329 Mile End Road and is the third oldest Jewish cemetery in England. It was first used in 1733 by the Sephardic community.

BRITISH MUSEUM   Great Russel Street

Tottenham Courtern Road Station (Northern Line)

The British Museum and British Library house one of the world's largest collections of Judaica. There are Torah scrolls from the now-vanished Jewish community in Kai-Feng Fu, in China, illuminated Bibles and Haggadahs, and priceless artifacts.

JEWISH MUSEUM (Woburn House)

Upper Woburn Place   Tel.388-4525

Euston Station (Victoria or Northern Line)

The Woburn House houses British Jewry's principal communal organizations. It also houses the United Synagogue, the Board of Deputies, the Chief Rabbi's office, and the court of the London Beth Din.

The Jewish Museum was opened in 1932. It houses ritual objects from old synagogues in London and throughout Europe. Some items of note include a Staffordshire jug depicting the boxing fight between a Sephardic Jew, Daniel Mendoza, and Richard Humphreys, in 1789. Mendoza defeated the previous champion and turned boxing into an art and was known as the "father of modern boxing."

There is a large gilded Ark which was discovered by a bookseller attending an auction sale at Chillingham Castle in Northumberland, where it had been used as a wardrobe in a servant's room. It was duly purchased and when restored, was found to date from the 16th century and to be of Italian origin, probably from a Venetian synagogue. The Jewish Museum is open Tuesday through Thursday (and Friday in the summer) 10:00 am. to 4:00 p.m. and on Sunday (and Friday in the winter) from 10:00 a.m. to 12:45 p.m.

Before entering the Woburn House, be prepared to undergo a security check.

MARBLE ARCH SYNAGOGUE

32 Great Cumberland Place

Marble Arch Station (Central Line)

This is the second home of the historic Great Synagogue on Duke's Place. The Duke's Place Synagogue was founded in 1690 by German or Ashkenazic Jews and was *the* synagogue of British Jewry, where all the community's major celebrations took place. It was built in 1790 but was destroyed by Nazi bombing raids in World War II.

The present synagogue is housed in a luxury housing complex near Marble Arch. It was not built as an independent structure.

HOLOCAUST MEMORIAL GARDEN

Marble Arch Station (Central Line)

The Holocaust Memorial Garden was dedicated in 1983. It is located in Hyde Park, near Marble Arch, in a section called the "Dell."

Be sure to go to Hyde Park on Sunday mornings.

WEST LONDON SYNAGOGUE

34 Upper Berkeley Street

Edgeware Road Station (District Line)

Designed in 1870 by the architectural firm of Davis and Emanuel, the West London Synagogue is one of the most glorious synagogue structures in England. It was organized in 1842 as a break from the Sephardic Bevis Marks Synagogue.

It was founded by the most prominent Jewish families in London - the Morcattas, Henriqueses, Montefiores, and the Goldsmids. The most luxurious materials were incorporated in the synagogue's design including Italian marbles for its columns and floor tiles, lavish mahogany paneling, and leather seats. The stained-glass windows depict exquisite floral designs.

The congregation follows the Reform ritual, which is similar to the Conservative Movement in the United States. The

Liberal Movement in Europe compares to America's Reform ritual. The congregation consists of 2,500 families.

WESTMINSTER SYNAGOGUE
Rutlands Gardens   Tel. 584-3953

Knightsbridge Station (Piccadilly Line)

The 1,564 Torah scrolls confiscated by the Nazis and stored in Prague, Czechoslovakia during World War II, were shipped to this synagogue in 1964. The Westminster Synagogue is housed in the former residence of Queen Victoria's father, the Duke of Kent. This synagogue has repaired many of these Torah scrolls and has shipped them to Jewish communities throughout the world. The Torah scrolls which are not sent out (on permanent loan) to needy congregations, are on display in the Westminster Synagogue.

CANARY WHARF PROJECT - THE DOCKLANDS
Britain's first skyscraper of American proportions is to form the centerpiece of the 12-million-square-foot Canary Wharf development proposed by Toronto-based developers Olympia & York for London's Docklands district (an area just east of the old East End section of London). Part of the project will include several hotels and the construction of a new underground link-up with the existing system.

The 800-foot-high, pyramid-topped building, designed by Cesar Pelli of New Haven, will be London's tallest. Pelli also designed the World Financial Center in New York's Battery Park City. Other parts of the $7 billion Canary Wharf project, which is billed as the world's largest commercial

Canary Wharf project near London's East End.

development, are designed by Kohn Pederson Fox of New York and the London and Chicago offices of Skidmore, Owings & Merrill.

Olympia & York is owned by the Reichman Brothers. They are Orthodox Jews and do not permit any work to be done on any of their multi-million-dollar projects during the Sabbath or on any Jewish Festival.

The Docklands Light Railway runs through this new project. Part of this new computerized railway line was built over a number of older lines built as early as 1840. The trains are automatically controlled from a central computer, which deals with all signalling and other safety factors, as well as adjusting speeds to keep within the timetable.

The major flaw with the new railway line is that the computers are constantly breaking down. It is therefore necessary for the Train Captain (conductor) to run the train "on manual."

The Docklands Light Railway can be picked up at Stratford (Central Line), Bow Road (District Line), or Tower Hill (District & Circle Line). Be sure to go to the last stop on the Docklands line - Island Gardens. Walk "under" the River Thames to Greenwich. Visit the National Maritime Museum and the original "Cutty Sark."

GOLDERS GREEN

Golders Green Station (Northern Line)

This suburb located in the northwest section of London, was built up following World War II. There are several large synagogues in the Golders Green, Hendon, Finchley area as well as many small *shtieblech.* Golders Green Road has the same Jewish atmosphere as Forest Hills and Borough Park, in New York. There are several Jewish gift shops and a variety of kosher restaurants and bakeries. One of the most popular Orthodox synagogues in Golders Green is Munk's Shul, located on a small street just off Golders Green Road, called The Riding.

The chassidic section of London is located in Stamford Hill. There is a Chabad (Lubavitch) House at 107-115 Stamford Hill (Tel. 800-0022). There are several Persian and Indian synagogues in this area.

LONDON MUSEUM OF JEWISH LIFE

The Sternberg Centre

80 East End Road   Tel. 346-2288

Fichley Central Station (Northern Line)

The London Museum of Jewish Life, founded as the Museum of the Jewish East End in 1983, is dedicated to the rescue and preservation of the social and cultural history of London's Jewish population. It is a community whose diverse roots stem from Sephardim who arrived with the readmission of 1656, Ashkenazim from Eastern Europe, refugees from Nazism and those, more recently, have fled from oppression in Iran and the Soviet Union.

The museum gathers objects, photographs, documents, and oral histories. There are exhibitions, educational programs, lectures, and walking tours. The museum is open Mondays through Thursdays, from 10:30 a.m. to 5:00 p.m. and on Sundays from 10:30 a.m. to 4:30 p.m. It is closed Friday, Saturday, and all Jewish Festivals.

Note: The Jewish Medical Emergency Service of London (Hatzolah) can be reached at 806-1123.

Manchester

JEWISH MUSEUM

190 Cheetham Hill Road   Tel. (061) 834-9879

The former Spanish and Portuguese Synagogue was built in 1873. Sir Albert Sassoon laid the cornerstone. The building is located in the old Jewish section of Manchester. That area is now predominantly Pakistani and black. The present Jewish community is located about a mile away in Prestwich and Salford. The Jewish population of Manchester is about 35,000. To the right of the Jewish Museum are sites of former synagogues. The United Synagogue was housed in a former church. Number 159 Cheetham Hill Road was the location of the Great Synagogue of Manchester. It was built in 1857 in the Neo-Classical style. That building has been standing in ruins for many years. The former New Synagogue and Beth Hamedrash is presently occupied by Simon & Simon Lamp Factory. The Stars of David still appear on the façade.

Oxford

OXFORD SYNAGOGUE

21 Richmond Road   Tel. 0865   53042

This synagogue is of comparatively recent origin compared with the tradition that the ancient in Oxford was built in 1227. It was located opposite what is now St. Aldate's Church. The ancient Jewish cemetery was located in the site of the Botanical Gardens, opposite Magdalen College.

It has been reported that at least three of the University's oldest buildings - Jacob's , Moyse's, and Lombard Halls - were built as Jewish homes in the 12th century. The first "coffeehouse" in England was opened in Oxford in 1650 by Jacob the Jew. It was located at 85 High Street. There is a memorial plaque which attests to this.

Oxford is the site of the Sir Isaac Wolfson College, which was created in 1965.

Plymouth

SYNAGOGUE

 Catherine Street   Tel.(0752) 66-16-26

The Plymouth Synagogue was built in 1761 and is the oldest Ashkenazic synagogue in England.

Ramsgate

MONTEFIORE SYNAGOGUE & MAUSOLEUM

The Synagogue in Ramsgate was built in 1833 by Sir Moses Montefiore, the renowned philanthropist. It was modeled after the Great Synagogue of Livorno (Italy), where he was born. Sir Moses Montefiore died at the age of 101. He designed the mausoleum for his wife, Lady Judith. It is located next to the synagogue and was designed as an exact copy of the Tomb of Rachel, who died on the road between Jerusalem and Bethlehem.

The synagogue has an exterior clock on its façade as well as the family crest of the Montefiores. It is located in the former lavish seaside resort of Ramsgate, which is located along the English Channel, just north of Dover. Today, the former Montefiore Estate has been sold to developers. There are new private condominiums being built along the "White Cliffs." The synagogue is still maintained and is located in a park-like setting, except the park is now overgrown with wild vegetation. The synagogue is not within walking distance from the railroad station. It is best reached by local taxi.

Rochester

ROCHESTER CATHEDRAL

There is a statue on the façade of this cathedral called the "Synagogue Defeated." It portrays a blindfolded woman carrying a shattered staff and holding an inverted Ten Commandment Tablets in the other hand. This cathedral was built in the mid-13th century. There are similar depictions of the "Synagogue Defeated" in Notre Dame (Paris), Strasbourg, and Rheims.

York

CLIFFORD'S TOWER

The Third Crusade inflamed the Christians against "infidel" Jews in their midst. Debtors seized the occasion of the current anti-Jewish feeling to cause riots and to burn the records of transactions in which they were involved.

The Jews fled into Clifford's Tower, the central tower of a medieval castle, built on a Norman mound. When the angry mobs broke into the tower, they found that many of the Jews had committed suicide. Those remaining alive were slaughtered on the spot. Yom Tov of Joigny, an eminent scholar from France, was living in York in 1190, and was among the Jews who committed suicide during the Festival of Passover, in Clifford's Tower. The tower is still there, but it is now in ruins.

SCOTLAND

Edinburgh

HEBREW CONGREGATION

4 Salisbury Road   Tel. 031-667 3144

The first records of Jewish settlement in Scotland date back to 1665. The first major community, however, was established around 1780. The first synagogue in Scotland was opened in 1816 in a lane near Nicholson Street. This was followed by its succeeding building on Richmond Court. The present synagogue dates from 1932 and is located at 4 Salisbury Road.

ANCIENT JEWISH CEMETERY   Calton Hill

The oldest Jewish cemetery in the country is located at the foot of Calton Hill. The oldest tombstone dates back to 1790. There is another Jewish cemetery located at 8 Braid Place. The oldest tombstone in that cemetery dates back to 1832.

Glasgow

GARNETHILL SYNAGOGUE

29 Garnethill Street   Tel. 041-332 4151

Overlooking the City of Glasgow is the most elegant synagogue in Scotland. Built in 1879 by architect Sir John McEwen, the synagogue resembles the West London Synagogue. The Ark is recessed into a skylighted apse. There are exquisite marble columns and floor tiles. The stained-glass windows depict beautiful floral patterns. The interior stained-windows behind the women's gallery is said to have come from an earlier synagogue in Scotland.

Sir Isaac Wolfson, the first Jew in Scotland to be made a peer, and Sir Maurice Bloch, whiskey-maker and philanthropist, were members of this synagogue. The synagogue is used only on the Sabbath and on Jewish Festivals as well as for special *simchas*. The Garnethill Synagogue is located in the old section of Glasgow. Most of the Jewish community has moved to the suburb community of Giffnock.

The Jews of Scotland were involved in the tobacco, clothing, furniture, and whiskey trades. The largest manufacturer of kilts was Denis Bonchy Cohen, of Glasgow.

WALES

Cardiff

UNITED SYNAGOGUE

Cathedral Road   Tel. 0222 229813

Glasgow's Garnethill Synagogue was built in 1879.

This congregation was founded in the 1840s. There are 4,000 Jews in Wales. The majority live in Cardiff.

Swansea

HEBREW CONGREGATION

Ffynone   Tel. 0792 206285

The first Jewish settlement in Wales traces its roots to the 1760s. The first synagogue was built in 1780. The present synagogue, however, was built in the 1950s to replace the synagogue on Goat Street which was destroyed in a Nazi air raid in 1941.

There are synagogues in Wales located in Bangor, Brynmawr, Colwyn Bay, Llandudno, Methyr Tydfil, Pontypridd, Porthcawl, Llanelli, Newport, and Rhyl.

KOSHER PROVISIONS

Bournemouth   New Ambassador Hotel   *Tel. 25453*

Hove   Cantor's Deli   *20 Richardson Road*   *Tel. 723-669*

Cambridge   Kosher Canteen   *Tel. 357-147*

Gateshead   (bakery)   *215 Coatsworth Road*   *Tel. 77201*

Leeds   (bakery)   *378 Harrogate Road*   *Tel. 691-350*

London

Aviv   *87 High Street*   *Tel. 952-2484*

Bloom's   *90 Whitechapel High Street*   *Tel. 247-6001*

30 Golders Green Road   *Tel. 455-3033*

Curzon Plaza Restaurant
56 Curzon Street (W1)   Tel. 071-499 4121 ext. 308
Dizengoff Restaurant
118 Golders Green Road   Tel. 081 - 458-7003

Grodzinski's Bakeries

Kaifeng *51 Church Road (Hendon) Tel. 081 203-7888*

L'Grana Restaurant
1-4 Belmont Parade, Finchley Road Tel. 081-455 0210

Pizza Pita *119 Golders Green Road Tel. 455-8921*

Reubens *20a Baker Street Tel. 935-5945*

Sami's *85 Brent Street Tel. 202-9247*

The White House

 10 Bell Lane (Hendon) Tel. 081 203-2427

Zizi's Chinese Restaurant
1023 Finchley Road Tel. 081-201 8777

Manchester

Fulda's Hotel *84 Bury Old Road Tel. 740-4551*

Deli King *Kings Road Tel. 798-7370*

Newcastle *101 St. George's Terrace Tel. 281-2838*

Sunderland Deli *14 Briery Vale Road Tel. 567-6341*

NORTHERN IRELAND

Belfast

Community Centre *49 Somerton Road Tel. 777-974*

(deli) *493 Antrim Road Tel. 777-462*

SCOTLAND

Edinburgh

(bakery) *84 East Crosscauseway Tel. 667-1406*

Glasgow

Freed's   *49 Coplaw Street   Tel. 423-8911*

(deli)   *200 Fenwick Road (Giffnock)   Tel. 638-8267*

(grocery)   *2 Burnfield Road   Tel. 638-4383*

SYNAGOGUES

ENGLAND

Birmingham

Ellis Street   Tel. 643-0884

133 Pershore Road   Tel. 440-4044

11 Park Road

4 Sheepcote Street   (Progressive)   Tel. 643-5640

Blackburn   *19 Clayton Street   Tel. 53834*

Blackpool

Leamington Road   Tel. 28614

Raikes Pde.   (Reform)   Tel. 32513

Bolton   *Central Street*

Bournemouth

Springhurst Road   Tel.27433

53 Christchurch Road   (Reform)   Tel. 34451

Bradford

Springhurst Road   Tel. 499-979

Manningham Lane   (Reform)   Tel. 28925

Brighton   *66 Middle Street   Tel. 27785*

Bristol

9 Park Row   Tel. 23538

43 Bannerman Road   (Progressive)   Tel. 541-937

Bromley   *28 Highland Road   Tel. 460-5460*

Cambridge   *Ellis Court & Thompson Lane*

Chatham   *High Street*

Cheltenham   *St. James Square*

Chingford   *Marborough Road*

Colchester   *Priory Street*

Coventry   *Barras Lane   Tel. 20168*

Crawley   *Langley Lane   (Progressive)*

Croydon   *30 Elmont Road   Tel. 684-4726*

Derby   *270 Burton Road*

Eastbourne   *22 Susans Road*

Epsom   *Prospect Place   Tel. 21150*

Exeter   *Mary Arches Street   Tel.51529*

Gateshead   *180 Bewick Road   Tel. 71338*

Greenford   *39 Lodfield Lane*

Grimsby   *Heneage Road*

Harlow   *Harnert's Road*

Harold Hill   *Trowbridge Road*

Harrogate   *St. Mary's Walk*

Hove

29 New Church Road

Holland Road

6 Lansdown Road   (Liberal)

Palmeira Avenue   (Reform)

Hull

Osborne Street

Park Street

Linnaeus Street   Tel. 228-252

Leeds

21 Newton Park View   Tel. 624-191

46 Spencer Place   Tel. 33304

1 Louis Street   Tel. 623-254

Winton Street

Reginald Terrace

Roman Avenue   (Reform)   Tel. 665-256

98 Chapeltown Road   Tel. 621-351

Belgrave Street

Chapeltown Road & Moortown

Leicester   *Highfield Street   (Progressive)   Tel. 832-927*

Letchworth   *15 Sollershott East*

Liverpool

Princes Road   Tel. 709-3431

Greenbank Drive   Tel. 733-1417

2 Dove Tale Road

Church Road North 15   (Liberal)   Tel. 733-5871

101 Ullet Road

Dunbabi Road   Tel. 722-2079

Mather Avenue   Tel. 427-6848

London

There are over one hundred congregations in the greater London area. For information regarding services and synagogue locations, you may contact the following organizations:

United Synagogue   Tel. 387-4300

Federation of Synagogues   Tel. 247-4471

Union of Orthodox Hebrew Congregations   Tel. 802-6226

Spanish & Portuguese Jews' Congregation   *Tel. 289-2573*

Liberal Synagogues   Tel. 580-1663

Reform Synagogues   Tel. 349-4731

Luton   *116 Bury Park Road   Tel. 25032*

Maidenhead   *9 Boyne Hill Avenue (Reform)   Tel. 73012*

Manchester

Cheltenham Cres.   Tel. 792-1233

Upper Park Road   Tel. 740-3905

Sunnybank Road   Tel. 766-7442

Leicester Road   Tel. 740-4830

453 Cheetham Hill Road   Tel. 740-7788

18 Moor Lane   Tel. 773-1344

Shay Lane   Tel. 980-6549

Middleton Road   Tel. 740-4766

Bury Old Road   Tel. 740-1210

Ribble Drive   Tel. 766-5986

62 Singleton Road   Tel. 740-1629

17 North Cumberland Street   Tel. 792-1313

Stenecourt & Holden Roads   Tel. 740-4027

Vine Street   Tel. 792-2413

132 Leicester Road   Tel. 792-2413

Bury New Road   Tel. 773-1978

14 Hesketh Road   Tel. 973-2172

Parkview Road   Tel. 773-6092

Old Lansdowne Road   Tel. 445-5731

Wilbraham Road   Tel. 224-1366

Meade Hill   Tel. 740-9586

Park Lane   Tel. 766-3732

Coniston Road   Tel. 428-8242

Atrinchan Toad   (Reform)   Tel. 980-7595

Jackson's Row   (Reform)   Tel. 834-0415

Elms Street   (Reform)   Tel. 796-5063

Margate   Godwin Road   Tel. 20964

Middlesborough   Park Road South   Tel. 819-590

Newcastle

Great North Road

37 Eskdale Terrace

Graham Park Road

Clayton Road   (Reform)   Tel. 842-502

Northampton   *Overstone Road*

Norwich   *3a Earlham Road   Tel. 23948*

Nottingham

Shakespeare Street   Tel. 42004

Lloyd Street   (Progressive)   Tel. 325-111

Oxford   *21 Richmond Road   Tel. 53042*

Peterborough   *142 Cobden Avenue   Tel. 71282*

Plymouth   *Catherine Street   Tel. 661-626*

Portsmouth   *The Thicket   Tel. 824-391*

Ramsgate   *Hereson Road*

Reading   *Goldsmith Road   Tel. 53954*

Romford   *25 Eastern Road*

Ruislip   *Shenly Avenue   Tel. 32934*

St. Albans   *Oswald Road   Tel. 54872*

St. Annes   *Orchard Road   Tel. 721-831*

Sale   *14 Hesketh Road   Tel. 2172*

Sheffield

Wilson Road   Tel. 360-299

127 Psalter Lane   Tel. 52296

Solihull   *3 Monastery Drive*

Southampton   *Mordaunt Road*   Tel. 773-647
Southend

Finchley Road

851 London Road   *(Reform)*   Tel. 76349

South Shields   *25 Beach Road*   Tel. 84508

Stoke   *Birch Terrace*   Tel. 641-116

Sunderland

Ryhope Road   Tel. 658-093

Monbray Road   Tel. 57417

Sutton   *14 Cedar Road*   Tel. 8029

Torquay   *Abbey Road*   Tel. 605-352

Watford   *16 Nascot Road*   Tel. 22755

Whitley Bay   *2 Oxford Street*   Tel. 521-367

NORTHERN IRELAND

Belfast   *49 Somerton Road*   Tel. 777-974

SCOTLAND

Aberdeen   *74 Dee Street*   Tel. 22135

Dundee   *St. Mary Place*   Tel. 28140

Edinburgh   *4 Salisbury Road*   Tel. 667-3144

Glasgow

20 Belleisle Street   Tel. 634-2001

29 Garnet Street   Tel. 332-4151

Maryville Avenue   Tel. 638-6600

125 Niddrie Road   Tel. 423-4062

Clarkson Road   Tel. 644-3611

147 Ayr Road   (Reform)   Tel. 639-4083

Beech Avenue   Tel. 639-2442

Faloch Road   Tel. 632-5025

WALES

Aberdare   *19a Seymor Street   Tel. 588-3586*

Cardiff

Cathedral Road

Penylan & Brandreth Roads   Tel. 483-959

Moira Terrace   (Reform)   Tel. 691-243

Llandudno   *Church Walk   Tel. 76848*

Merthry Tydfil   *Church Street   Tel. 3113*

Swansea   *Ffynone Street   Tel. 207-146*

MIKVEHS

ENGLAND

Birmingham   *Bourrnille Lane Baths   Tel. 440-1019*

Bournemouth   *Wooton Gardens   Tel. 27433*

Brighton   *Church Street   Tel. 685-6952*

Gateshead   *180 Bewick Street   Tel. 773-047*

Leeds   *368 Harrogate Road   Tel. 685-119*

Leicester   *Highfield Street Shul   Tel. 700-130*

Liverpool   *Dundabin Road   Tel. 722-2079*

London   *40 Queen Elizabeth Walk (N.16)   Tel. 802-6226*

Manchester

Broome Holme & Tetlow Lane   Tel. 792-3970

Sedgley Park Road   Tel. 773-1537

Southport   *Arnside Road   Tel. 32964*

Westcliff   *Genesta Road   Tel. 44900*

NORTHERN IRELAND

Belfast   *49 Somerton Road*   *Tel. 777-974*

SCOTLAND

Glasgow   *Maryville Avenue*   *Tel. 638-6600*

WALES

Cardiff   *Wales Empire Pool Building*   *Tel. 22296*

RAILROAD TIMETABLE

London to: Amsterdam............. 8:15 - 17:35

Belfast...................... 10:30 - 22:25

Berlin....................... 9:15 - 6:28

Copenhagen............ 9:15 - 9:17 (next day)

Glasgow.................. 7:45 - 13:02

Paris......................... 9:45 - 17:50

Rome....................... 9:45 - 10:05 (next day)

Venice...................... 9:45 - 7:14

Vienna..................... 9:15 - 9:50 (next day)

FINLAND

Finland's first Jewish settlers came to the country in 1830 - against their will! They were the so-called Cantonists or "Nicolaievskis," young Jewish boys, between the ages of 12 and 25 years, who had been drafted into the Russian army for a period of twenty five years, and who were assigned to garrison duty in remote outposts of the Czarist empire, such as Finland and Siberia. The harsh conscription law had been designed during the reign of Czar Nicholas I, as a means of alienating the Cantonist (Jewish) child recruits from their own people and religion and forcing their conversion to the Russian Orthodox Church. Each Jewish community within the Pale of settlement was assigned its quota of young draftees. There were special Jewish officers who carried out this task. They were known in Yiddish as *Chappers*, or kidnappers.

These were the boys who would become, twenty-five years later, the first Jewish settlers in Finland. Assigned to garrison duty in Helsinki or Viipuri, on the Russian border, many chose to stay in Finland when their quarter-century of service had ended.

Until Finland gained its independence in 1917, the Jews were subjected to severe restrictions, limiting their places of residence, curtailing their freedom of movement, and narrowing the occupations open to them to such enterprises as the peddling of second-hand clothes.

During the Russo-Finnish War in 1939, virtually every able-bodied Jew enlisted in the Finnish army. Although Finland became an ally of Nazi Germany in 1941, she refused the Nazi's request to turn over to them the German-Jewish refugees and resisted all anti-Jewish measures. Some Jews in the Finnish army were, for a time, actually part of the German army on the Finnish-Russian border.

There are today about 1,300 Jews in Finland.

Helsinki

GREAT SYNAGOGUE

Malminkatu 26   Tel. 60-03-86

The only synagogue in the city was built in 1906. There is a wreath presented to the congregation on the occasion of a visit by Field Marshal Mannerheim, in 1944. It is preserved in a glass case. The wreath memorializes the twenty-three Jewish soldiers who died in the Russo-Finnish War.

AHVENANMAA (ALEND) ISLANDS

These islands, located in the Gulf of Bothnia, contain the ruins of Bomarscund, a Russian fortress built partly by Jewish military conscripts. It was destroyed by British and French naval forces during the Crimean War in 1854. Nearby, are the graves of a number of Russian-Jewish soldiers.

KOSHER PROVISIONS

Helsinki

Finnkosher (deli) Uudenmaankatu 28   Tel. 644-951

(grocery) Malminkatu 36   Tel. 694 16 51

Rabbi Schwartz   Tel. 694 23 24

SYNAGOGUES

Helsinki

Malminkatu 26   Tel. 60-03-86   or 69-41-302

Turku

Brahenkatu 17   Tel. 12557

RAILROAD TIMETABLE

Helsinki to: Copenhagen .... 7.32 - 8.21   (next day)

Gothenburg .... 7.02 - 5.00

Hamburg ....7.32 - 15.01   (next day)

Oslo .... 7.32 - 7.55   (next day)

Stockholm ....7.00 - 19.45

FRANCE

There is evidence of Jewish settlement in ancient Gaul (today's France) dating back to the 4th century. The period between the 9th and 12th century marked a "Golden Age" for French Jewry. It was an era of the greatest rabbis and their world-renowned rabbinical academies. It was a period of cultural awakening, producing great scholars and poets. The first known scholar was Rabenu Gershom ben Yehudah (ca. 960-1030), who later was known as the *Meor ha-Golah,* the "Light of the Diaspora." He was responsible for issuing special ordinances, *takkanot,* which were designed to raise the level of morality. The most widely known of these *takkanot,* forbids polygamy. The achievements of Rabenu Gershom were continued by his disciple, Rabbi Shlomo Yitzchaki, generally known by his Hebrew acronym "Rashi." Though he studied in Worms, Germany, he was born, worked, and died in Troyes, France (1040-1105).

From the 11th through the 18th century, there were very explosive periods for the Jews. The first major upheaval occurred in 1096, with the First Crusade. The Christians aimed their attacks against the Jews living in the provinces which bordered the Rhine River. There were persecutions based on the accusation of "ritual murders." In 1240, the church condemned the writings of the Jews and publicly burnt editions of the Talmud. There were retaliatory expeditions organized by religious fanatics who accused the Jews of being the cause of the general poverty. In 1348, during the epidemic of the Black Plague, which took the lives of over one third of the population of Europe, some twenty-four million people, Jews were burned at the stake in many Alsatian towns, a persecution which is still commemorated in the name of several streets, especially in Strasbourg. During these massacres, the most heroic among the Jews committed collective suicide while others converted to Christianity.

In 1394, Charles VI expelled all Jews from France. This decree did not include Alsace, Contat Venaissin (Provence), and the County of Nice. It was not until 1784 that Jews were to return and settle in all parts of France. In 1791, the Jews were proclaimed full citizens of France. Napoleon assembled seventy-one Jewish leaders as a *Sanhedrin* in 1806, which was to clarify the Jewish attitude on the subject of the relations between church and state. This body was the forerunner of today's Consistorial system.

Many Jews achieved fame in France after the French

Revolution. In art, great names include Pissaro, Soutine, Bonheur, Pascin, Chagall, and Modigliani. Musical enrichment came from Jacques Offenbach, Claude Kahan, and Darius Milhaud. In literature and the humanities, Nobel Prize winners include Henri Bergson and Rene Cassin; notables in finance include the Rothschilds; in government, three French Prime Ministers include Leon Blum, Rene Meyer, and Pierre Mendes-France.

During World War II, over 100,000 French Jews were deported to the concentration camps. This group consisted primarily of Ashkenazic Jews. The majority of this group was annihilated. Following the war, many of the former Jewish communities were struggling to survive. In the 1960s, there was a major influx of Jews from the North African countries of Algeria, Morocco, and Tunisia. These were Sephardic Jews. They took-over the old and dying-out Jewish communities throughout France and virtually brought them back to life. Today, there are approximately 750,000 Jews in France, with 270,000 residing in Paris. Every Sunday morning at 9:15 a.m. there is a Jewish television program. It is hosted by Rabbi Josy Eisenberg and is on station Antenne 2.

Avignon

GHETTO SITE   rue Petite-Reille

The ancient ghetto was located near the Palace of the Popes. An ancient synagogue foundation was found near rue Pente-Rapide. The "New" ghetto was established in 1226 and was located along rue Jacob, place Jerusalem, and chemin de la Synagogue.

CALVET MUSEUM

65 rue Joseph Vernet   Tel. 90-86-33-04

This museum contains several artifacts which contain Judaic inscriptions.

Bayonne

BASQUE MUSEUM

1 rue Marengo   Tel. 59-59-08-98

The Basque Museum contains a *Salle Israelite* or Jewish Room. There are several religious artifacts including the coat-of-arms of wealthy ancient Jewish families of Bayonne.

ANCIENT SYNAGOGUE REMAINS

There are two locations which were originally ancient synagogue in Bayonne. They are at 49 rue Maubec (Temple de Gueldes) and at 22 place de la Republique (Temple Brandon). The latter was closed in 1872.

The present synagogue is located near the railroad tracks, at 35 rue Maubec. It was built in 1837, under the rule of King Louis Philippe.

JEWISH CEMETERY

The present cemetery is located in the St.-Etienne section of St.-Esprit. It was established in 1660.

Bordeaux

CHURCH OF ST. SEURIN

There is a statue of the Synagogue Defeated on the left side of the south portal.

Note: See notes on Notre Dame of Paris.

ANCIENT JEWISH QUARTER   rue Judaique

There is a *rue Porte-Dijeaux* or Jew's Gate. This was the gateway which entered into the ancient Jewish quarter.

GREAT SYNAGOGUE

8 rue Grand Rabbin Joseph Cohen   Tel. 91-70-39

This synagogue is one of the largest and most majestic Sephardic synagogue in all of France. It was built in 1882 as an Ashkenazic synagogue. During World War II, the Nazis and their French cohorts gutted the interior of the synagogue. The synagogue was used as a deportation center before the Jews were sent off to the extermination camps.

The synagogue was restored following the war. Seating capacity is about 1500. There is a magnificent gilded menorah in front of the bimah which stands 15 feet tall. Today, the congregation is Sephardic, with most of the congregants coming from North African countries in the 1960s.

Great Synagogue of Bordeaux was built in the 1880s.

Cannes

The city known for its annual international film festival and fireworks displays (nightly in mid-August) has a Jewish population of about 2,000. The synagogue , located at 19 boulevard d'Alsace was built in 1955 by an Egyptian Jew. The little domed synagogue is located just west of the railway station. Cannes' Jewish Community Center is located at 3 rue de Bone (Tel. 93-99-24-95).

Be sure to visit Juin-les-Pins in the summer. There are many Sephardic Jews, a kosher restaurant/grocery, kosher pizza shop and a synagogue. Please note that the kosher eateries are open only during the summer season.

Carpentras

SYNAGOGUE   place de la Synagogue

Originally built in 1367, the Carpentras Synagogue was remodelled in 1741 by architect Antoine d'Alemand. He originally had planned to construct the remodelled building 72 feet high. The church authorities were opposed to this height since it would be taller than both the Church of the White Penitents and the Cathedral of St. Suffrein. The walls of the synagogue were not to exceed 42 feet in height and the eastern windows which faced the church were walled up.

The synagogue is decorated in the delicate style of salons during the reign of Louis XV. The layout of the synagogue is quite unique. The Ark is on the main level, along the eastern wall. On the right side of the Ark, standing in a niche six feet above the floor, is a miniature Chair of Elijah. Decorated with appropriate inscriptions, the chair is symbolic of the Prophet Elijah protecting the new-born male child on the day of his circumcision. There was no tevah or reading platform on the main level, rather, it was placed on the upper gallery, in the women's section, along the western wall, and is reached by two sets of winding stairs on each side of the supporting Tuscan columns. In the original 1367 synagogue building, the women were placed in the cellar. There was a special rabbi or cantor who conducted the service for the women. The cellar also housed a matzoh bakery, complete with oven, grindstone, and a marble kneading table dated 1652. On an even lower level was a mikveh, the *cabussadou* as it was called in the Provençal dialect.

Note: There is a direct bus to Carpentras from the railroad terminal in Avignon. It is about a 40-minute ride. The Carpentras Synagogue is located opposite the Town Hall. It is open daily from 10:00 a.m. to 12 noon and from 3:00 to 5:00 p.m. There are daily and Sabbath services. There are about 100 families, the majority coming from North Africa.

Cavaillon

SYNAGOGUE   rue Hebraique, near rue Chabran

This synagogue is very similar in design to the Carpentràs Synagogue. There is, however, more extensive art-work in this synagogue, especially its delicate wrought-iron grilles and sculpted medallions. The synagogue also functions as a museum. It is open daily (except Tuesday) from 10:00 a.m. to 12 noon and from 2:00 to 5:00 p.m. If the building is closed, contact Mr. Mathon at 23 rue Chabran or Mr. Palombo at 36 rue Raspil (Tel. 78-02-46).

Luneville

SYNAGOGUE   5 rue Castara   Tel. 373-08-07

The synagogue built between 1785 and 1789 at Luneville reflects the elegance of 18th century France. Its façade, like that of a small but very superior urban residence, is ornamented with a discreetly Judaic symbol entirely in keeping with Neo-Classical taste - festoons of vine leaves and grapes.

Marseille

The coastal region along the Mediterranean Sea, stretching from Marseille to the Italian border at Ventimiglia is known as the French Riviera. There have been Jews in the region since Roman times. The largest city in the Riviera is Marseille. There are about 70,000 Jews living in Marseille. There are 20 synagogues, several yeshivot and kosher restaurants. There are two Jewish community centers: Centre Edmond-Fleg, 4 impasse du Dragon (13006 Marseille), Tel. 91-37-42-01; La Rose, 31 avenue des Olives (13010 Marseille), Tel. 91-70-05-45.

GREAT SEPHARDIC SYNAGOGUE
117 rue Breteuil   Tel. 81-13-57

This is the largest synagogue in the city. It was built in 1865 and was badly damaged during World War II. It houses the

Consistoire of Marseille. Most of the Jewish community in Marseille are recent immigrants. They arrived in the 1960s, following the civil wars in North Africa.

Monaco - Monte Carlo

There is a synagogue at 15 avenue de la Costa. Several years ago, there was an attempt to organize another congregation, due to constant disagreements among the members. The monarchy declared that there will not be two congregations within his kingdom. The congregation settled its arguements and is still under only one roof.

There is a kosher butcher at 70 avenue Saint Laurent (Tel. 30-11-73)

Nice

There were Jews living in Nice as early as the 4th century. In 1723, there was a ghetto in the heart of the old city. It is said that the house at 18 rue Benoit Bunico was originally an ancient synagogue.

Today, there are eight synagogues in Nice, which has a Jewish population of about 25,000.

GREAT SYNAGOGUE   7 rue Gustave Deloye

The Great Synagogue was built in the 1890s in Romanesque Revival style. The Ark was designed similar to the ones found in ancient Italian synagogues . The black marble Ark contains a walk-in room which houses fifteen Torahs, both Sephardic and Ashkenazic. During the summer season, the synagogue is packed - standing room only!

There is a small Ashkenazic synagogue just around the corner at 1 rue Blacas. It is run by the Lubavitch chassidim.

NATIONAL MUSEUM BIBLICAL MESSAGE OF MARC CHAGALL

Docteur Menard avenue & Cimiez boulevard

The most important permanent collection ever assembled and devoted to Marc Chagall is located in Nice. The museum is located in Cimiez, Nice's ancient Roman quarter. It includes large paintings, preparatory sketches, gouaches, and engravings. There are also lithographs, sculptures, stained-glass, and tapestries. For further information call 81-75-75.

Be sure to visit the medieval town of St. Paul-de-Vence and the Maeght Foundation, where a vast collection of modern sculpture and painting is housed in a striking modern building. Marc Chagall moved here in 1966 and lived in a house in the woods behind the Maeght Foundation.

For a lovely ride on a private railway, be sure to catch a train leaving from the Chemins de Fer de la Provence. It leaves from Nice and goes through the French Maritime Alps to Digne. You can catch a connecting bus and then another train which continues on to Grenoble.

Paris

Note: Paris Metro (subway) stations are in parentheses.

THE PLETZEL   (Metro #1 to Saint Paul)

Located on the site of the 13th century ghetto of Paris, known as the *Juiverie*, the Pletzel (Yiddish term for "little place") is still an active Jewish neighborhood. Jews have lived and worked for many centuries in these narrow streets. At one time, place Saint Paul was known as "Jews Place." At the turn of the 20th century, the area was populated mostly by Eastern European Jews. Yiddish was heard on the streets of the quarter and most of the signs in the store windows were printed in Yiddish as well. Since the last war, most of the old Ashkenazic shops have been replaced with Sephardic and Oriental owners. This change came about during the 1960s, after the civil wars in the north African countries. The dominant shop signs are now printed in French and Hebrew.

RUE PAVEE SYNAGOGUE

rue Pavee, near rue des Rosiers

(Metro #1 to Saint Paul)

This synagogue is the only one in Paris which was designed in the *art nouveau* style. Hector Guimard, the noted architect who designed the Paris Metro, was commissioned to design a synagogue in the Pletzel for Orthodox Jews who had just arrived from Eastern Europe. The synagogue was built in 1911 on a narrow site. It is four and a half stories in height, is designed in precast concrete forms, has two levels of balconies for the women, contains living quarters for the caretaker, and contains a Talmud Torah, offices, and community rooms. It has been declared a national historic landmark.

TEMPLE VICTOIRE

44 rue de la Victoire   (Metro #7 to le Peletier)

This austere and magnificent structure is often called the "Cathedral" and "Rothschild" Synagogue. It was designed by Alfred Philibert Aldrophe, in 1874. It was built in the days of Napoleon III in the Romanesque Revival style. Originally, the plans called for the synagogue to have its main façade along rue St. Georges, a more conspicuous entrance on a major boulevard. The empress's confessor suggested that the synagogue should not be visible from such a thoroughfare. Therefore, the temple was built on the side street and its Ark is therefore not in the proper orientation. The temple's construction was financed by the Rothschilds. It is lavishly decorated with marble and stained-glass and is dominated by glorious candelabras. The two chairs on either side of the Ark are reserved for the Chief Rabbi of France and the Chief Rabbi of Paris. For information about services call 40 82 26 26.

CONSISTOIRE OF PARIS

17 rue Saint-Georges   (Metro #7 to le Peletier)

This is the headquarters of the Jewish community of Paris, officially known as the Association Consistoriale Israelite de Paris. It was created by an ordinance on May 25, 1844, which

Synagogue, rue de la Victoire (1865-1874)

fixed the compositions of the consistories. For further information about the Jewish community of Paris call 40 82 26 26.

NOTRE DAME CATHEDRAL   (Metro #4 to Cite´)

On either side of the main portal of the cathedral are two raised statues of women. The statue on the left side of the main portal represents the "Church Triumphant. " It is wearing the crown she has taken from her enemy. The statue on the right side of the main portal is called the "Synagogue Defeated." It is portrayed as a blind-folded woman, her staff is shattered, and the Tablet of the Law is slipping from her hand. Her crown has been removed and is on the floor by her feet.

Notre Dame Cathedral was constructed during the 13th century. It was during this period in which severe anti-Semitic acts were perpetrated against the Jews throughout Europe. Many of the Gothic Cathedrals built during this period display these two opposing statues on their façades, such as Amiens, Bordeaux, Strasbourg, Rheims (France) , and Lincoln and Rochester (England).

MEMORIAL TO THE DEPORTED
(Metro #4 to Cite´)

Located in a garden behind Notre Dame Cathedral on the tip of the *Ile de la Cite´*, not far from the Pletzel. This memorial is dedicated to the 200,000 French men and women of all races and religions who died in the German death camps during World War II. The memorial was designed by architect Georges-Henri Pingusson in 1962.

MEMORIAL TO THE UNKNOWN
JEWISH MARTYR

17 rue Geoffroy-l'Asnier (Metro #7 to Pont-Marie)

One of the most moving Jewish memorials in Paris is a tribute to the six million Jews who perished in the Holocaust. It was dedicated in October, 1956. A huge bronze cylinder in the center of the courtyard is designed in a shape symbolizing a crematorium urn and has the names of the notorious concentration camps engraved on its surface. Along the wall of the courtyard are seven bronze plaques which were designed by Arbit Blatas. There are similar Holocaust memorial plaques designed by the same artist located within the walls of the ancient Ghetto of Venice and near the United Nations, in New York City, in Dag Hammarskjold Park.

The museum contains documents and photographs relating to the war. It is open daily, except Saturday, from 10:00 a.m. to 12 noon and from 2:00 to 5:30 p.m. For further information call 227-44-71.

MUSSEE DE CLUNY

6 place Paul Painleve   (Metro #10 to Saint Michel)

The Cluny Museum contains the Strauss-Rothschild collection of Jewish ritual objects. There are Jewish engagement rings, sculptures, and attached to the wall, are a series of stone slabs which were originally 13th century Jewish tombstones. There is also an inscribed cupboard Ark and reading desk, *tevah*, which have come from a 15th century synagogue in Modena, Italy.

JEWISH ART MUSEUM

42 rue des Saules

(Metro #12 to Lamarck-Caulaincourt)

Located in the shadow of the Sacre Coeur Basillica, the Jewish Art Museum of Paris contains rare exhibits of detailed models of Eastern European wooden synagogues from the 12th century, collections of Jewish ritual art, paintings by Chagall, and other famous Jewish artists. It also contains drawings, etchings, sculpture, and mosaics. The museum is open Sunday, Tuesday, and Thursday from 3:00 to 6:00 p.m. For further information call 257-84-15.

MUSSEE DU LOUVRE   (Metro #1 to Louvre)

The Louvre contains many Jewish archaeological items and antiquities from Israel. The Palestine Room of the Sully Crypt contains a special gift from the late General Moshe Dayan of Israel. It is a terra cotta ossuary discovered in a funeral cave in Azor, near Tel Aviv.

The Art and Furniture department of the Louvre contains a collection of antique furniture and jewelry presented by Baron Adolph de Rothschild in 1900.

ROTHSCHILD MANSIONS

rue du Faubourg-St.-Honore

(Metro #9 to St. Phillipe du Roule)

There are several exquisite mansions which, at one time, belonged to several members of the Rothschild family. They are located along rue du Faubourg-St.-Honore, at numbers 33, 35, 41, 45, and 49.

POMPIDOU CENTRE

rue Beaubourg   (Metro #11 to Rambutteau)

The Pompidou Centre is a 21st century art museum. Its design is still controversial. All of the building's guts - mechanical, air conditioning, plumbing, and heating pipes and ducts are exposed on the outside of the structure and are painted in bright reds, greens, blues, and yellows!

The museum exhibits paintings by the Jewish artists: Chagall, Soutine, and Mondigliani. The museum also contains numerous books on Jewish history, Judaica, Israel, and Jewish literature. The Pompidou Centre, which is visited by about 25,000 persons daily, is not far from Notre Dame Cathedral and the Pletzel.

Take the glass-enclosed exterior escalator up to the roof of the museum and see an exciting panoramic view of Paris. There are continuous "street performances" below, in the plaza in front of the Pompidou Center.

JEWISH COMMUNITY CENTRE

19 boulevard Poissonniere

(Metro #8 to rue Montmartre)

There are dances, movies, classes, some sports, Saturday evening socials for singles, and Wednesday evening Israeli folk dancing. The center also houses a kosher cafeteria and serves lunches from 12 noon to 2:00 p.m. There is a synagogue on the premises. For further information call 233-64-96.

Note: The Jewish Community Center is closed during the

month of August. There are additional Jewish community centers which have kosher cafeterias throughout Paris: Centre Edmond Fleg, 8 bis, rue de l'Eperon (75005 Paris), Tel. 46-33-43-24; Centre Rachi, 30, boulevard de Port Royal (75005 Paris), Tel. 43-31-98-20; Centre Rambam, 19-21, rue Galvani, (75017 Paris), Tel. 45-74-52-80; Merkaz de Montmartre, 42, rue des Saules, (75018 Paris), Tel. 46-06-71-39.

CEMETERIES

Napoleon granted equal rights to all the people under his rule. This equality was during their lives as well as after death. The cemeteries of Paris are non-sectarian. Jews and Christians are buried in the same cemetery. The largest and most popular cemetery which people visit is the Cimitiere du Pere Lachaise. Some notable figures buried here include Oscar Wilde, Sarah Bernhardt, the Rothschilds, Camille Pissarro, Paul Dukas, and the Jewish auto manufacturer, Andre Citroen. Be sure to purchase a small map and directory at the gate-house. The nearest Metro station is Pere Lachaise, on the #2 or #3 Line.

The Montmartre Cemetery (Metro #2 to Blanche) contains the remains of Emile Zola, Heinrich Heine, and Jacques Offenbach. Note: This cemetery is two blocks from the world-renowned Moulin Rouge.

Colonel Alfred Dreyfus is buried in the Montparnasse Cemetery. The nearest Metro station is Raspail, on the #4 or #6 Line.

Before Napoleon designated equality to all citizens, the Jews buried their dead in their own Jewish cemeteries. There is an old Sephardic cemetery located at 44 rue de Flandres. This cemetery was closed in 1810. There are still about thirty tombstones. The old Ashkenazic cemetery is located at 96 rue Gabriel Peri, south of the Porte d'Orleans. It was closed in 1809. Permission to see these two old Jewish cemeteries must be received from the Paris Consistoire, located at 17 rue St. Georges (Tel. 526-02-56).

Side Trips

For those who are daring and adventuresome, there is a tour of the sewers of Paris. This tour leaves from the Pont de l'Alma, on the corner of Quay d'Orsay. For information about this unique tour call 47-05-10-29.

There is also another interesting off-the-beaten-tracks tour of Paris. You can see the catacombs of Paris in the old quarries. This tour leaves from 2 place Denfert Rocheran. You must bring your own flashlight! For further information call 43-22-47-63.

There is another 21st century-type-museum. It is the new Cite´des Sciences et de l'Industrie. This is a science and industry museum designed for children. There are exciting space-ships hanging from the five-story-high ceiling. There are also many "hands-on" exhibits. The museum is located in the northeast section of Paris. The nearest Metro station is Porte de la Villette, on the #7 Line.

If you take the R.E.R (express subway line) to the station called "Defense" you will step out into a plaza with 21st century-style office buildings. These state-of-the-art structures have won many architectural awards.

A special warning about the "man-eating" turnstiles in some of the older Metro stations. They consist of two tall gates that open hydraulically for only five seconds after you insert your yellow Metro ticket. If you are carrying a bulky item such as luggage, you will most probably get stuck between those two gates, since they open and close within only five seconds, not enough time for anyone to pull a bulky item through! The gates have rubber edges but they do not have any safety devices. The only way to get out of that situation is if someone else inserts another yellow Metro ticket. So beware! Note: The Eurailpass is not accepted on any subway, bus, or trolley line in any city in Europe. It is only good for most inter-city railroad lines.

Provence

In the southern part of France during the medieval period, groups of Jews lived in the four "Holy Communities:" Avignon, Carpentras, Cavaillon, and l'Isle-sur-Sorgue, in what was then papal territory. It was to this region where the Pope had been exiled in the 14th century. Jews in this region spoke the Provençal dialect and adhered to the Sephardic ritual, adding a special liturgy of their own, call *comtadin,* which greatly resembled Portuguese. Living under the direct jurisdiction of the popes, they fared better than the Jews in the rest of France. This does not mean, however, that they escaped arbitrary restrictions and expulsions directed at other Jews in France. The Jews served as financiers and merchants. No medieval synagogues have survived in France, but two

18th century synagogue buildings at Carpentras and Cavaillon have been restored following World War II and declared national monuments. Today, they are maintained as museums as well as functioning synagogues.

In 1990, the ancient Jewish cemetery in Carpentras was desecrated. Several tombstones were toppled and a recently-buried body was disinterred. There were spontaneous protests and demonstrations throughout France.

Saarebourg

SYNAGOGUE   12 rue du Sauvage   Tel. 703-12-67

There were periods in French Jewish history when the Jews were restricted in their design of the synagogue. It was not to be a tall structure (taller than the cathedral). The Jews wanted to subdue their synagogue design by having the building "blend-in" with the neighboring structures. At times these synagogues resembled barns and were actually known as *stahl* or barn synagogues. This camouflaged appearance might one day actually save the synagogue from angry mobs during pogroms. The synagogue in Saarebourg was built in 1858 on the site of an earlier and smaller building. The exterior looks similar to the adjoining barn. During World War II, the Nazis used this synagogue as a wharehouse. The interior, having been restored after the war, is a gem, complete with its marble Ark, exquisite stained-glass windows, and brass candelabras.

Strasbourg

Jewish history in Strasbourg goes back to the 12th century. There were savage persecutions during the Crusades and many massacres over the centuries. From the 14th century to the French Revolution, Jews were not permitted to live in Strasbourg. Rue Brulee memorializes the massacre of February 13, 1349, when 2,000 Jews were burnt in a huge bonfire for refusing to accept baptism. The City of Strasbourg today is known as the "Jerusalem of France." It is an active and highly organized intellectual Jewish community which has supplied many of the chief rabbis of France. Today, there are about 12,000 Jews living in Strasbourg.

ALSATIAN MUSEUM   23 quai St. Nicolas

The Alsatian Museum contains a rich collection of Jewish ritual objects. They are displayed in three rooms on the main floor. This collection belongs to the Jewish Museum.

SYNAGOGUE DE LA PAIX

1A rue du Grand Rabbin Rene Hirschler Tel. 88-35-61-35

The main synagogue, replacing the one destroyed by the Nazis during World War II, was built in 1958. It was designed by architect Meyer Levy. Twelve sixty-foot high columns support the segment-arched copper barrel-roof. The Ark, a cylindrical structure with a conical roof, is derived from the shape of a rolled-up scroll of the Law. The various types of wood from former French African colonies are used in the door fittings. The southern aisle of the main sanctuary leads

Great Synagogue of Strasbourg

out into an open pillared portico, which overlooks a beautiful public park. Seating capacity is seventeen hundred. A bronze menorah and a bronze grating shaped in the pattern of a Star of David grace the front of the structure.

There are two additional chapels in the adjoining community center; one is used by a Sephardic congregation, the other is used as a children's congregation. There is a kosher restaurant in the basement of the building.

STRASBOURG CATHEDRAL

On the south portal of the Strasbourg Cathedral is a statue depicting the Synagogue Defeated. The statue is represented by a blindfolded figure and shorn of her mantle. Note, this statue is not on the main or front façade of the cathdedral but rather on the right side of the massive structure. There is only one tower because the congregation ran out of funds to complete it several centuries ago. There is a *rue des Juifs* located behind the cathedral. This was the site of of medieval Jewry.

There is another representation of the Synagogue Defeated on the front façade of the Eglise Catholique Saint-Pierre le-Vieux. It is located just seven minutes from the railroad terminal, on the way to the Strasbourg Cathedral.

MUSEUMS

The following museums contain objects and exhibits of Jewish interest:

Aix-en-Provence

Musee Granet,   *13 rue Cardinal, Tel. 42-38-14-70*

Arles

Arlesian Museum, *42 rue de la Republique*

Lapidary Museum, *Place de la Republique*

Musee d'art chretien, *7 rue Baize*

Chalon-sur-Saone

Musee Denon, *place de l'Hotel-de-Ville, Tel. 85-48-01-70*

Dijon

Musee archeologique, *rue de Dr-Maret, Tel. 80-30-88-54*

Nancy

Musee historique Lorrain,

64 Grande Rue et place Ducale, Tel. 83-32-18-74

Narbonne

Musee de Narbonne,

place de l'Hotel-de-Ville, Tel. 68-32-31-60

Nimes

Musee archeologique,

Boulevard de l'Amiral-Courbet, Tel. 66-67-25-57

Orleans

Musee historique d'Orleans,

Square de l'Abbe-Desnoyers

Toulouse

Musee des Augustins,

21 rue de Metz, Tel. 61-22-29-22

Side Trips

For a truly breathtaking and unforgetable journey go to Chamonix and take the cable car *over* Mont Blanc, Europe's tallest mountain (15,772 feet). You can continue across the Italian border to Courmayeur. You will see mountain-climbers, skiers, spectacular ice-rivers, and even rock-slides and avalanches. There is one part of the cable-car ride where the cabins stop in mid-air, suspended two thousand feet above a glacier. Another part of this journey feels as if the cables are snapping, and the cabin drops twenty feet in three seconds. This is truly a journey to remember.

Note: This cable car ride operates only during the summer

season. Allow three hours for your journey up and an additional three hours for your return trip. The summer season is when everyone comes to Chamonix for this experience.

If you plan to cross the English Channel from Dover to Calais or some of the other cross-points in Belgium or England, be sure that the Channel is calm. If there are rough seas you will regret taking the ferry. If the seas are rough, definitely, do not take the hovercraft! It is like being in an airplane with extremely rough turbulence- for a continuous forty-five minutes.

The first phase of the English Channel Tunnel, commonly known as the "Chunnel," was completed in the end of 1990. There will be three tubes. Two will be used to transport high-speed trains. The third tube will act as a service tunnel in case of an emergency. Two types of trains will operate in the Chunnel. One train will carry only passengers. The other train will carry only cars, trucks and buses. The ride through the Chunnel will be so short that people will remain in their cars while sitting piggy-back in the train (on two tiers).

When the Chunnel will be completed, a train ride from Paris to Dover, England will take only three hours. The TGV train will operate on a new line directly from Paris. The problem will be once the passengers reach England. England does not have any plans to construct a high-speed rail line from Dover to London, so it will take an additional two hours to get to London from the English Channel.

While in France, be sure to take a ride on the fastest train in

Europe, the T.G.V. It departs from the Gare de Lyon in Paris. It is not as fast as Japan's "Bullet Train" but it does reach a maximum speed of 185mph. France is expanding TGV service in all parts of the country in conjunction with the "open market" plan of 1992. The Eurailpass is accepted on the T.G.V. but a reservation is necessary and a small surcharge (of about $2.00) is required.

Other countries which are constructing high-speed rail lines include Spain, Italy, Switzerland and Germany.

KOSHER RESTAURANTS

Aix-les-Bains

Auberge de la Baye Hotel

Chemin du Tir aux Pigeons   Tel. 79-88-07-01

Cannes

Hotel Acapulco   *16 boulevard d'Alsace   Tel. 93-99-16-16*

Lyon

Lippman   *4 rue Tony Rollet   Tel. 78-42-49-82*

Marseille

Centre Communautaire Edmond Fleg

4 Impasse du Dragon   Tel. 91-37-42-43

Chez Max

11 rue Combalat   Tel. 91-37-89-04

Le Petit Caveau

4 rue Mazagran   Tel. 91-48-72-79

Mount Carmel

5 rue de l'Arc   Tel. 91-33-42-13

Pitapain Tchick Tchak

65 rue d'Aubagne   Tel. 91-54-45-33

Prest Pizza Cash

rue Gaston Berger   Tel.   (91)   75-19-00

Metz

Restaurant Galil - Centre Communautaire

39 rue du Rabbin Elie Bloch   Tel. 87-75-04-44

Nancy   Centre Communautaire

19 boulevard Joffre   Tel. 83-32-10-67

Nice

Restaurant King Georges

26 rue Pertinax   Tel.   93-13-07-99

Le Roi David

9 rue Clement Roassal   Tel. 93-87-65-25

Paris

Adolphe   *14 rue Richer   Tel. 47 70 91 25*

Allo Kemia   *38 rue Curiel   Tel. 40 35 08 98*

Aux Iles Philippine   *17 rue Laplace   Tel. 46 33 18 59*

Aux Surprises

40 bis rue du Fg Poissonniere   Tel.   47 70 55 96

Azar & Fils   *6 rue Geoffroy Marie   Tel. 47 70 08 38*

Bendosa   *1 rue Saulnier   Tel. 42 03 14 69*

Berbeche Burger   *47 rue Richer   Tel. 47 70 81 22*

13 av Edourd Branly   (Sarcelles)   Tel. 34 19 12 02

Blue Bird   *27 Blvd de Charonne   Tel. 40 09 71 98*

91 av Secretan   Tel. 42 39 50 41

Cafe Joseph   *122 Blvd de Clichy   Tel. 45 22 45 21*

Cash Food   *63 rue des Vinaigriers   Tel. 42 03 95 75*

Centre Communautaire

19 Blvd Poissonniere   Tel. 42 33 64 96

8 rue de 8 Mai 1945 (Creteil)   Tel. 43 77 01 70

Centre Edmond Fleg   8 bis rue de l'Eperon   Tel. 46 33 43 31

Centre Rachi   30 Blvd de Port Royal   Tel. 43 31 98 20

Chalom   10 rue Richer   Tel. 42 46 77 70

Chez Francois   5 rue Ramponeau   Tel. 47 97 87 28

Chez Gabin   92 Blvd de Belleville   Tel. 43 58 78 14

Chez Shlomi   2 rue Geoffroy Marie   Tel. 47 70 37 31

Chicken Cash   4 rue Malher   Tel. 05 05 22 00

China Glatt   56 rue Richer   Tel. 42 46 01 19

Douer Restaurant   21 rue Bergere   Tel. 45 23 53 22

Douieb   11 bis rue Geoffroy Marie   Tel. 47 70 86 09

Du Cote de Chez Fred

17 rue Micolon   (Alfortville)   Tel. 48 93 55 37

Eilat's Food   8 rue Geoffroy Marie   Tel. 42 46 39 56

Elygel   116 bolvd de Belleville   47 97 09 73

Georges de Tunis   40 rue Richer   Tel. 47 70 43 77

Habiba   3 ter rue des Rosiers   Tel. 48 87 39 73

Hattab le Tun   8 rue du Passage St. Martin   Tel. 42 06 42 77

Hotel Lebron   4 rue Lamartine   Tel. 48 78 75 52   Open Shabbat

John Burger   24 rue Richer   Tel. 48 00 96 48

Juliette   14 rue Duphot   Tel. 42 60 18 05

King Salomon   46 rue Richer   Tel. 42 46 31 22

Kol Bo   17 av du 8 Mai 1945   (Sarcelles)   Tel. 39 94 06 47

L'Atikva   3 Cour des Petites Ecuries   Tel. 47 70 67 07

La Halav'vite   26 bis rue de l'Ourcq   Tel. 40 34 40 84

La Palme d'Or   22 Blvd des Filles du Calvarie   43 55 28 17

La Parnassa   53 Blvd Montparnasse   Tel. 45 44 97 47

La Petite Famille   32 rue des Rosiers   Tel. 42 77 00 50

La Rose Blanche   *10 bie rue Geoffroy Marie   Tel. 45 23 37 70*

La Toasterie   *48 rue Richer   Tel. 47 70 24 19*

Le Bambou d'Eilat   *2 rue de Nantes   Tel. 40 37 19 14*

Le Castel   *4 rue Saulnier   Tel. 47 70 44 08*

Le Cabourg   *102 blvd Voltaire   Tel. 47 00 71 43*

Le Cotel

   5 Blvd Henri Poincarre   (Sarcelles)   Tel. 39 92 42 38

Le Cristal   *11 rue Montyon   Tel. 42 46 21 65*

Le Gros Ventre   *7 rue Montyon   Tel. 48 24 25 34*

Le Laguna

   8 rue d'Estienne d'Orves   (Creteil)   Tel. 42 07 10 38

Le Lotus de Nissan   *39 rue Amelot   Tel. 43 55 80 42*

La Manhattan   *231 Blvd Voltaire   Tel. 40 09 09 14*

Le Castel Restaurant

Restaurant gastronomique

Sous le contrôle du Beth-Din

4, rue Saulnier, 75009 PARIS   Tel. 47. 70. 44. 08

(Beth Din of Paris)

Le Massada

12 Place de France Flanades   (Sarcelles)   Tel. 39 90 15 98

Le Nouveau Magenta (Hollywood Pizza)

73 Blvd Magenta   Tel. 48 24 70 24

Le Renaissance   *4 rue Biscornet   Tel. 43 43 17 06*

Le Roll's Pizzeria   *56 av de la Republique   Tel. 43 38 63 18*

126 Blvd Voltaire   Tel. 48 06 53 46

Le Shalom   *231 Blvd Voltaire   Tel. 43 48 29 32*

Le Taket's   *54 rue Richer   Tel. 48 24 96 05*

Les Ailes   *34 rue Richer   Tel. 47 70 62 53*

Les Jardins de Belvedere   *111 av de Villiers   Tel. 42 27 16 91*

Les Flames en Roses

122 rue de Paris   (Montreuil)   Tel. 48 58 51 03

Les Jardins de Nazareth

44 rue ND de Nazareth   Tel. 42 78 98 22

Les Relais   *69 Blvd de Belleville   Tel. 43 57 83 91*

Les Tables de la Loi   *2 rue d'Hauteville   Tel. 40 22 90 69*

Les 3 J   *64 av Jean Jaures   (Pantin)   Tel. 48 91 34 82*

Luminieres de Belleville

102 Blvd de Bellville   Tel. 47 97 51 83

Maguena

40 Blvd Albert Camus   (Sarcelles)   Tel. 34 19 40 45

Mazal Tov   *25 rue des Rosiers   Tel. 40 27 87 40*

Mitsou Yan   *18 Fg Montmartre   Tel. 45 23 02 22*

Natania   *27 rue Poissonniere   Tel. 48 40 13 80*

New Beauegard   *18 rue Baeuregard   Tel. 42 36 66 30*

Ness Cachere   *3 rue Henri Ribiere   Tel. 42 41 99 71*

Nini   *24 rue Saussier Leroy   Tel. 46 22 28 93*

Or El *17 rue Montyon Tel. 48 24 06 57*

Paparon Follies *17 rue Richer Tel. 47 70 81 97*

Paris Texas *101 av Jean Jaures Tel. 42 45 48 61*

Patrick *11 rue Montyon Tel. 47 70 21 20*

Patrick Gourmet (salon thé)

      25 rue de Trévise Tel. 48 01 04 55

Pekanti *26 rue de l;Ourcq Tel. 40 35 73 68*

Pita Burger *53 rue ND Nazareth Tel. 42 78 13 12*

      26 rue des Rosiers 42 77 59 41

      21 rue de Fg Montmartre Tel. 42 77 04 13

Resto Flash *10 rue Lucien Sampaix Tel. 42 45 03 30*

Snack Quick Delight *34 rue Richer Tel. 45 23 05 12*

Sidney *8 rue de la Grange Bateliere Tel. 47 70 05 02*

Tibi *128 Blvd de Clichy Tel. 45 22 96 99*

Zazou *19 rue Fg Montmartre*

Note: Jo Goldenberg's is not kosher but serves
      kosher-style meals.

Strasbourg

Chalom *1a rue Rene Hirschler*   *Tel. 88-36-56-30*

 Le Domino *28 rue Sellenick*   *Tel. 88-35-15-04*

Restaurant Universitaire

      11 rue Sellenick Tel. 88-35-59-57

Toulouse Aux Cornes de Gazelle

      4 rue Jules Chalande Tel. 61-22-60-38

GROCERIES & KOSHER PROVISIONS

Aix-les-Bains

Yarden *58 Rue de la Liberation Tel. 50-92-64-05*

26 rue Pertinax
06000 NICE
TÉL. 93 13 07 99

The King of Kosher Cuisine

Come and discover the friendly atmosphere in our elegant restaurant. We serve the most delicious cuisine in the French Riviera.

Open for Shabbat - Reservations Required

Under the Supervision of the Grand Rabbinate of Nice.

DAVID GUEZ

58 Avenue Jean Médecin
06000 Nice France

Catering Facilities Available for All your Simchot

PASSOVER on the French Riviera

MERIDIEN HOTEL **** Nice

Prestigious Hotel
French Gastronomic Cooking
Glatt Kosher   *Entertainment*

Supervised by "Nice" French Riviera Beth Din

Information & Reservations:

David Guez
58 Avenue Jean Médecin
06000 Nice France

Tel. 33 93 80 73 94
or 33 93 80 73 96
or 33 93 54 93 90
FAX 33 93 13 96 04

Antibes/Juin les Pins

A. Krief (snack bar) *13 av. L. Galet   Tel. 93 67 50 61*

Sebbah (butcher) *28 rue Maizieres   Tel. 93 34 60 11*

Zanna (butcher)

21 av. du Docteur Dautheville   Tel. 93 67 44 55

Beziers   Chemouni   *19 rue de l'Argenterie*

Grenoble   Barukh Sala   *49 rue Thiers*

Lille

Centre Communautaire *5 rue Auguste Angellier*

Lyon

Central Cash

   105 Grande Rue de la Guillotiere   Tel. 78-72-47-61

 Masliah Bakery

   151 ter, rue Joliet Curie   Tel. 78-36-82-78

Marseille

Colbo Market   *16 rue Chevalier Roze   Tel. 91-90-75-15*

Metz

Cacher Centre   *10 rue des Jardins   Tel. 87-75-28-41*

Nice

Maison Guez *28 rue Pertinax*

Orleans

Centre Communautaire   *14 rue Robert de Courtenay*

Strasbourg

Casher Center

            12 boulevard Poincarré   Tel. 88-32-25-55

Bakery & Grocery

            4 rue Strauss Durekheim   Tel. 88-35-68-21

SYNAGOGUES

Agen *52 rue Montesquieu* *Tel. 96-17-79*

Aix-en-Provence *3 rue de Jerusalem* *Tel. 26-69-39*

Aix-les-Bains *rue du President Roosevelt*

Amiens *38 rue du Port d'Amont* *Tel. 89-66-39*

Angers *12 rue Valdemaine*

Annency *18 rue de Navrick* *Tel. 67-69-37*

Antibes/Juin-les-Pins

  Villa la Monada *Chemin des Sables* *Tel. 93 61-59-34*

Arcachon *Cours Desbey* *(summers only)*

Arles *7 chemin de Barrol*

Avignon *2 place de Jerusalem* *Tel. 25-12-92*

Bastia *3 rue de Castagno* *Tel. (95) 31-58-82*

Bayonne *35 rue Maubec* *Tel. 55-85-41*

Belfort *6 rue de l'As de Carreau* *Tel.28-55-41*

Besançon *2 rue Mayence* *Tel. 80-82-82*

Beziers *19 place Pierre Semard* *Tel. 28-75-98*

Biarritz *rue de Russie* *(High Holy Days only)*

Bischeim *place de la Synagogue* *Tel. 33-02-87*

Bitche *28 rue de Sarreguemines*

Bordeaux

8 rue du Grand Rabbin Joseph Cohen *Tel. 91-70-39*

Boulay *rue du Pressoir* *Tel. 779-20-34*

Bourges *66 rue Charlet*

Brest *8 quai de la Douane* *Tel. 45-98-42*

Caen *46 avenue de la Liberation* *Tel. 93-46-32*

Cagnes sur Mer *5 rue des Capucines*

Cannes *19 boulevard d'Alsace* *Tel. 93 38-16-54*

Carpentras   *place de la Synagogue*

Cavaillon   *rue Hebraique   Tel. 78-02-46*

Chalon-sur-Marne   *21 rue Lochet   Tel. 68-09-92*

Chalon-sur-Saone   *10 rue Germigny   Tel. 48-05-41*

Chambery   *44 rue Saint Real*

Clermont-Ferrand   *6 rue Blatin   Tel. 93-36-59*

Colmar   *1 rue de la Cigogne   Tel. 41-38-29*

Creil   *1 place de la Synagogue   Tel. 425-16-37*

Dijon *5 rue de la Synagogue   Tel. 66-46-47*

Draguignan   *15 rue de l'Observance   Tel. (93) 68-41-45*

Dunkerque   *19 rue Jean Bart   Tel. 66-92-66*

Elbeuf   *rue Gremont   Tel. 81-19-61*

Epernay   *2 rue Placet   Tel. 51-26-83*

Epinal   *9 rue Charlet   Tel. 82-25-23*

Evian   *Avenue des Crottes*

Frejus Saint-Raphael   *rue du Progres   Tel. 94 52-06-87*

Grasse   *82 route de Nice   Tel.   (93) 36-05-33*

Grenoble   *11 rue Andre Maginot   Tel. 87-02-80*
                4 rue des Bains

Haguenau

rue du Grand Rabbin Joseph Bloch   Tel. 93-87-24

Juin-les-Pins/Antibes

   Villa la Monada   *Chemin des Sables   Tel. 61-59-34*

Le Havre   *38 rue Victor Hugo   Tel. 21-14-59*

Hyeres   *Chemin de la Ritorte   Tel.   (94) 65-31-97*

Le Mans   *4 boulevard Paixbans   Tel. 31-99-55*

Lens   *87 rue Casimir Beugnet   Tel. 28-22-14*

Libourne   *33 rue Lamothe   Tel. 51-45-99*

Lille   *5 rue August Angelliers   Tel. 52-41-59*

Limoges   *25 rue Pierre Leroux   Tel. 77-47-26*

Luneville   *5 rue Castara   Tel. 373-08-07*

Lyon

16 rue Siant Mathieu   Tel. 800-72-50

la Sauvegarde & la Duchere   Tel 835-14-44

317 rue Duguesclin   Tel. 858-18-74

13 quai Tilsitt   Tel. 837-13-43

47 rue Montesquieu

60 rue Crillon

11 rue Saint Catherine

Marseille

119 rue Breteuil   Tel. 37-49-64

8 impasse Dragon   Tel. 53-33-73

24 rue Montgrand   Tel. 33-61-79

14 rue Saint Dominique   Tel. 39-64-30

31 avenue des Olives   Tel. 70-05-45

57 boulevard Barry   Tel. 66-13-15

134 boulevard Michelet

27 boulevard Bonifay   Tel. 89-40-62

18 rue Beaumont   Tel. 50-30-57

205 boulevard Daint Marguerite   Tel. 75-63-50

15 avenue des 3 Freres Carasso   Tel. 66-70-42

20 chemin Saint Marthe   Tel. 75-14-97

60 chemin Vallon de Toulouse   Tel. 75-14-97

Menton   *106 cours du Centenaire   Tel. (93) 28-56-32*

Metz   *39 rue du Rabbin Elie Bloch   Tel. 775-04-44*

Monaco   *15 avenue de la Costa   Tel. 93 30-16-46*

Montpelier *5 rue des Augustins   Tel. 60-49-93*

Mulhouse *19 rue de la Synagogue   Tel. 45-85-41*

Nancy *17 boulevard Joffre Tel. 332-10-67*

Nantes *5 impasse Copernic   Tel. 73-48-92*

Nice

Great Synagogue *7 rue Gustave Deloye   Tel.   (93) 92-11-38*

1 rue Blacas   (Ashkenazic) Tel. 62-38-68

8 rue Marceau   Tel. 85-82-06

22 rue Michelet Tel. 51-89-80

boulevard des Moulins, Tour 40 St. Augustin   Tel. 52-06-88

23 Avenue E. Ripert   Tel. 54-97-57

39 Boulevard du Parc Imperial   Tel. 96-83-12   (Kollel)

1 rue Boissy d'Anglais   Tel. 80-58-96

31   Avenue Henri Barbusse   Tel. 51-43-63

9 Avenue A. Theuriet   Tel. 98-47-89

25 Avenue du Val Marie   Tel. 21-10-69

22 Avenue Rossini   Tel. 88-42-78   (Lubavitch)

Nimes

40 rue Roussy

12 rue Emile-Jamais

Obernai   *rue de Selestat*

Orleans   *14 rue Robert de Courtnay*

Paris

<u>2e arrondissement</u>

19 boulevard Poisonnieres   (Sephardic) Tel. 42 33 64 96

<u>3e arrondissement</u>

15 rue Notre-Dame de Nazareth   Tel. 42 78 00 30

Group Rabbi Yehiel de Paris

25 rue Michel-Leconte   Tel. 42 78 89 17

Nettzach Israel Ohel Mordehai

5 rue Sainte-Anastase   *Tel. 43 07 40 34*

4e arrondissement

Tefilat Israel Frank Forter

24 rue Bourg-Tibourg   *Tel. 42 78 08 37*

18 rue des Ecouffes   *Tel. 48 87 97 86*

Agudas Hakehilos   *10 rue Pavée*   *Tel. 48 87 21 54*

Oratoire Mahzike Adath Mouvement Loubavitch

17 rue des Rosiers

25 rue des Rosiers

21 bis, rue des Tournelles   *Tel. 42 74 32 80*

14 place des Vosges   *Tel. 48 87 79 45*

Tifereth Israel   *44 rue Vielle du Temple*   *Tel. 48 99 82 06*

5e arrondissement

Seminaire Rabbinique   *9 rue Vauquelin*   *Tel. 47 07 21 22*

Centre Rachi   *30 boulevard du Port-Roya*   *Tel. 43 31 98 20*

6e arrondissement

Centre Edmond Fleg   *8 bis, rue l'Eperon*   *Tel. 46 33 43 24*

7e arrondissement

27 avenue de Ségur   *Tel. 47 83 60 33*

8e arrondissement

Hekhal Moshe   *218 rue du Fbg-St-Honoré*

9e arrondissement

Rachi Chul   *6 rue Amboise-Thomas*   *Tel. 48 24 86 94*

28 rue Buffault   *Tel. 45 26 80 87*

Rav Frankforter   *10 rue Cadet*   *Tel. 42 46 36 47*

Berith Chalom   *18 rue Saint-Lazare*   *Tel. 48 78 45 32*

Beth El   *3 rue Saulnier*   *Tel. 47 70 09 23*

Beth Israel   *4 rue Saulnier   Tel. 40 22 94 40*

Rothschild Synagogue   *44 rue de la Victoire   Tel. 40 82 26 26*

Beth Loubavitch   *8 rue Lamartine   Tel. 45 26 87 60*

Tiferet Yaacob   *71 rue de Dunkerque   Tel. 42 81 32 17*

Kollel Rav Levy

37 boulevard de Strasbourg   Tel. 42 46 07 74

10e arondissement

4 rue Martel

9 rue Guy-Patin   Tel. 42 85 12 74

37 boulevard de Strasbourg   Tel. 42 46 07 74

13 rue des Petites-Ecuries   Tel. 42 46 65 02

75 rue du Fbg St-Martin

130 rue du Fbg St-Martin   Tel. 42 05 85 05

"Rav Pealim"   *49 boulevard de la Villette   Tel. 42 41 55 44*

11e arrondissement

Etz Haim   *18 rue Basfroi   Tel. 43 48 82 42*

Don Isaac Abravanel   *84 rue de la Roquette   Tel. 47 00 75 95*

Ora Vesimha   *37 rue des Trois-Bomes   Tel. 43 57 49 84*

Ozar Hatorah   *40 rue de Lorillon   Tel. 43 38 73 40*

108 avenue Philippe Auguste

12e arrondissement

Beth Yaacov   *15 rue Lamblardie   Tel. 43 47 36 78*

Fondation Rothschild Oratoire

76 rue de Picpus   Tel. 43 44 78 10

13e arrondissement

19 rue Domrémy   Tel. 45 85 25 56

61 rue Vergniad   Tel. 45 88 93 84

66 avenue d'Ivry   Tel. 45 85 94 39

14e arrondissement

6 bis, villa d'Alésia

Association Cultuelle Israelite

121 rue de l'Ouest   Tel. 45 40 88 40

223 rue Vergingetorix   Tel. 45 45 03 43

15e arrondissement

14 rue Chasseloup-Laubat   Tel. 42 73 36 29

Ohel Merdekhai   *13 rue Fondary   Tel. 45 79 91 97*

16e arrondissement

Ohel Abraham   *31 rue Montevideo   Tel. 45 04 66 73*

23 bis, rue Dufrénoy   Tel. 45 04 94 00

6 bis, rue Michel-Ange   Tel. 45 20 00 08

5 bis, rue Montévidéo   Tel. 45 03 42 93

17e arrondissement

Centre Rambam   *19 rue Galvani   Tel. 45 74 51 81*

Beth Hamidrach Lamed   *10 rue Barye   Tel. 40 53 91 57*

18e arrondissement

80 rue Doudeauville   Tel. 46 06 12 24

13 rue Sainte-Isaure   Tel. 42 64 48 34

42 rue des Saules   Tel. 46 06 71 39

Adar Israel   *5 rue Duc*

19e arrondissement

Ohr Thora   *15 rue Riquet   Tel. 40 38 23 36*

Bet Chalom   *11 rue Curial   Tel. 40 37 65 16*

Collel Hamabit   *21 rue Barbanegre   40 38 13 59*

Ecole Lucian de Hirsch   *70 avenue Secrétan   Tel. 42 08 84 14*

Ohr Yossef   *29 rue de Thionville   Tel. 42 00 84 46*

Beth Loubavitch   *25 rue Riquet   Tel. 40 36 93 90*

Chaare Thora   *1 rue Henri-Turot   Tel. 42 06 53 71*

Centre Loubavitch   *53 rue Compans   Tel. 42 02 20 35*

54 avenue Secétan   Tel. 42 08 57 26

59 rue de Flandre   Tel. 40 35 06 94

Rabbi David ou Mosché   *45 rue de Belleville   Tel. 40 18 30 63*

Ohalei Yaacov   *11 rue Henri Murger   Tel. 42 49 25 00*

25 rue des Solitaires   Tel. 42 02 98 95

56 rue Darius Rihaud

Kollel Ysmah Moché   *36 rue des Annelets   Tel. 43 63 73 94*

20e arrondissement

120 boulevard de Belleville   Tel. 47 97 46 96

75 rue Julien-Lacroix   46 36 30 10

17 rue de Cour-des-Noues   Tel. 43 58 14 70

Beth Yaacov Yossef   *43 rue Saint-Blaise   Tel. 43 56 03 11*

19 rue de Tourtille Machmia-Chalor   Tel. 47 97 75 20

Beth Habad   *84 rue des Couronnes   Tel. 43 49 15 34*

Beth Habad   *93 rue des Orteaux   Tel. 40 24 10 60*

50 bis, rue des Praires   Tel. 43 66 35 27

Maor Athora   *16 rue Ramponneau   Tel. 40 21 31 29*

Note: There are an additional 140 congregations in the surrounding suburbs of Paris.

Pau   *8 rue des Trois Freres Bernadac   Tel. 62-37-85*

Perigueux   *13 rue Paul Louis Courrier   Tel. 09-57-50*

Perpignan   *54 rue Arago   Tel. 34-75-81*

Reims   *49 rue Clovis   Tel. 47-68-47*

Roanne   *9 rue Beaulien   Tel. 71-51-56*

Rouen   *55 rue des Bons Enfants   Tel. 71-01-44*

Saarebourg   *12 rue de Sauvage   Tel. 703-12-67*

Sarreguemines *rue Georges V   Tel. 798-20-48*

St. Etienne *34 rue d'Arcole   Tel. 33-09-18*

St. Fons *17 avenue Albert Thomas   Tel. 867-39-78*

St. Laurent du Var

   Villa "Le Petit Clos" *35 av. des Oliviers   Tel. 93 31 63 63*

St. Louis *19 rue du Temple*

St. Quentin   *11 boulevard Henri Martin Tel. 62-17-36*

Selestat *4 rue Saint Barbe   Tel. 92-04-35*

Sete *quai d'Orient   Tel. 53-24-13*

Strasbourg

1a rue Rene Hirschler   Tel. 35-61-35

2 rue St. Paul le Jeune

rue d'Istanbul

6 rue de Champagne

rue Rieth

28 rue Kageneck

1 rue Silvermann

Tarbes   Cite Rothschild

6 rue du Pradeau   Tel. 93-04-74

Tarbes *6 rue du Pradeau*

Thionville *31 avenue Clemenceau   Tel. 253-23-23*

Toulon

6 rue de la Visitation   Tel. 91-61-05

avenue Lazare-Carnot

Toulouse

14 rue du Rempart, St. Etienne Tel. 61-21-69-56

2 rue Palaprat   Tel. 61-62-90-41

17 rue Alsace Lorraine Tel. 61-21-51-14

35 rue Jules Chaland

8 rue Etienne Colongues Colomiers

Tours *37 rue Parmentier Tel. 05-56-95*

Troyes *5 rue Brunneval Tel. 43-11-02*

Valence *1 place du Colombier Tel. 43-34-43*

Valenciennes *36 rue de l'Intendence Tel. 33-49-13*

Verdun *impasse des Jacobins Tel. 84-30-51*

Versailles *10 rue Albert Joly Tel. 951-05-35*

Vichy *2 bis rue du Marechal Foch Tel. 98-44-02*

Villeurbanne

4 rue Malherbe Tel. 884-04-32

40 rue Alexandre-Boutin

13 rue Chevreuil

Chemin Cyprian

Rue du Dr. Frappaz

MIKVEHS

Aix-en-Provence *3 rue de Jerusalem Tel. 26-69-39*

Aix-les-Bains

rue Roosevelt (Pavilion Salvador) Tel. 35-38-08

Avignon *rue Guillaume Tel. 85-21-24*

Bordeaux *213 rue St. Catherine Tel. 91-79-39*

Cannes Beth Esther *20 blvd d'Alsace Tel. 93 38 16 54*

Colmar *3 rue de la Cigogne Tel. 41-38-29*

Dijon *5 rue de la Synagogue Tel.65-35-78*

Grenoble *11 rue Andre Maginot Tel. 87-02-80*

Haguenau *7 rue Neuve*

Lens *58 rue du Wets Tel. 28-16-16*

Lyons

18 rue Saint Mathieu   Tel. 800-72-50

317 rue Duguesclin   Tel. 858-18-74

40 rue Alexandre Boutin   Tel. 824-38-91

Marseille

Colel   *43a Ch. Vallon de Toulouse   Tel. 75-28-64*

Longchamp   *45a rue Consolat   Tel. 62-42-61*

Redon   *13 boulevard du Redon   Tel. 75-58-49*

Beth Myriam   *60 Chemin Vallon de Toulouse   Tel. 75-20-98*

Metz   *rue Kellerman   Tel. 775-04-44*

Mulhouse   *19 rue de la Synagogue   Tel. 45-85-41*

Nantes   *5 impasse Copernic   Tel. 73-48-92*

Nice   *22 rue Michelet   (93) 51-89-80*

1 rue Boissy d'Anglais   80-17-94

Nimes   *40 rue Roussy   Tel. 23-11-72*

Paris

176 rue du Temple   (75003)   Tel.42 71 89 28

50 rue Lacépede   (75005)   Tel. 45 35 26 90

50 Faubourg St. Martin   (75010)   Tel. 42 06 43 95

19 rue Galvani   (75017)   Tel. 45 74 52 80

31 rue des Thionville   (75019)   Tel. 42 45 74 20

1 rue des Amelets   (75019)   Tel. 42 40 10 26

25 rue Riquet   (75019)   Tel. 40 36 40 92

75 rue Julien-Lacroix   (75020)   Tel. 46 36 39 20

Saint Louis   Institut Messilat Yesharim

Vielle route de Hagenthal   Tel. 68-51-77

Sarreguemines   *rue Georges V   Tel. 798-20-48*

Strasbourg   *1a rue Rene Hirschler   Tel. 36-43-68*

Toulon   *6 rue de la Visitation   Tel. 91-61-05*
Toulouse   *15 rue Francisque Sarcey   Tel. 61-21-20-32*
Troyes   *5 rue Brunnevalid   Tel. 43-11-02*

RAILROAD TIMETABLE

Paris to: Amsterdam.................. 10:23 - 16:34
             Barcelona..................... 9:33 - 23:31
             Berlin........................... 7:30 - 20:46
             Copenhagen............... 7:30 - 22:45
             Lisbon.......................... 9:00 - 9:55 (next day)
             London....................... 7:55 - 13:50
             Madrid......................... 20:00 - 8:55
             Marseille..................... 10:11 - 15:06
             Nice............................. 10:11 - 18:06
             Rome........................... 7:34 - 23:55
             Stockholm................... 7:30 - 8:17 (next day)
             Venice......................... 7:18 - 19:34
             Vienna........................ 7:45 - 22:50
             Zurich.......................... 7:00 - 13:57

GERMANY

The first Jews to reach Germany were merchants who went there in the wake of the Roman legions and settled in the Roman-founded Rhine towns. The earliest detailed record of a Jewish community in Germany, referring to Cologne, is found in imperial decrees issued in 321. There was no continuous Jewish settlement in Germany until the 10th century. Jewish traders from Italy and France settled in Speyer, Worms, and Mainz. These three cities, known as *Shum* (an abbreviation based on the initial letters of the Hebrew names of these cities), were to become great centers for Jewish education. Among the many noted rabbis of this "Jerusalem of Germany" were Rabbi Gershom ben Yehudah (known as the "Light of the Diaspora," *Me'or ha Golah*), who established a seminary for Talmudic studies in Mainz around the year 1000, and one of his disciples, Rabbi Shlomo Yitzchaki (commonly referred to as Rashi), who lived in Troyes, France, but attended the yeshiva in Worms, Germany.

For three centuries, the Jewish communities of Germany prospered. In 1096, the First Crusade began. It heralded the process of disintegration which gathered momentum throughout the Middle Ages. Before long, it lead to the persecution of the Jews, which has continued ever since, century after century, in the form of blood libels and burnings at the stake. The Jews were never expelled from the whole of Germany (as in France, Spain, and Portugal) since it was not yet united. The Jews would move to another "land," sometimes only a few miles away, which offered them a temporary haven. Nevertheless, many thousands of Jews died as martyrs, refusing to save themselves (as the Spanish and Portuguese Jews) through baptism. This "*kiddush ha Shem,*" the idea of self-sacrifice, of becoming a martyr rather than apostasy, and of standing up to the attacker, were formulated and transmitted as permanent principles. A special blessing was inserted into the prayer book, to be recited by those who were about to be slain.

The Jews of Germany were gradually impoverished, reduced to peddling, confined to ghettos (as in Frankfurt-am-Main), and deprived of all civic rights. They were required to wear special yellow badges and Jews hats, *Judenhutten.*

It was not until the 17th and 18th centuries that Jews were invited back to help repair the destruction wrought by the Thirty Years' War. Jews then became members of the royal courts, financiers, and counselors to the nobility. This was the Age of Enlightenment, which was to change the status and image of the Jews in Germany. It was also this *Haskalah* (Enlightenment) which ushered in the Reform and Liberal movements. It was the French Revolution which granted even greater freedoms to the Jews.

In 1870, the tides turned against the Jews when the country was flooded with anti-Semitic literature, whose underlying theme was the racial superiority of Aryans and the inferiority of Semitic peoples. Hitler continued this campaign against the Jews, culminating in his "final solution," resulting in the murder of more than six million Jewish men, women, and children.

There are about 34,000 Jews in West Germany, with 6,000 living in West Berlin and about 1100 living in East Germany. There are many Israelis and Russian Jews living in West Germany.

Altenkunstadt (Lichtenfels district)

SYNAGOGUE   Judenhof 3

The synagogue built in the first half of the 18th century, with a rabbi's apartment in the building, will be restored in 1991.

Ansbach

SYNAGOGUE MUSEUM

Located in the old medieval section of the city, the Ansbach Synagogue was built in 1746 by the Court Jews who owed their loyalty to the Margrave Karl Wilhem Frederick. He commissioned an Italian architect, Leopold Retti, who designed it in the Italian Baroque style. The Jews were well-liked by all the local citizens. It was because of this benevolence that the synagogue was spared from destruction. On November 9, 1938, the Nazis burned hundreds of synagogues as a reprisal for the killing of a German diplomat by a Jew in Paris. Thousands of Jews were arrested and the windows of Jewish-owned stores were shattered, hence the name, "Night of the Broken Glass," or *Kristallnacht*, in German. When the Gestapo approached the synagogue in Ansbach, the mayor of the city refused to obey the order to torch the synagogue. He rather took several wet rags, placed them inside the synagogue, near the windows, and ignited them. There was much smoke but no real fire. The Gestapo was convinced that the synagogue was truly burning and continued on their way.

An ederly Christian neighbor saw the smoke emanating from the synagogue, quickly ran inside and rescued the Torahs from the "fire." She hid them in her house but did not tell anyone where they were stored. The elderly women passed away during the war and took her secret with her. To this day, nobody knows where the ancient Torahs are located!

The Ansbach Synagogue is one of the only synagogues in

Germany that was not destroyed during the war. There are no Jews living in Ansbach today. The ancient synagogue has been restored and is now a museum. It can be visited by contacting Mr. Adolphe Lang, the city archivist, in the Ratthaus. Mr. Lang lives in the nearby town of Bechofen. He is trying to restore the ancient Jewish cemetery in that town. The old wooden synagogue of Bechofen had exquisite murals designed by the itinerant Jewish artist, Eliezer Sussman. That synagogue was totally destroyed on Kristallnacht. The prominent and respected doctor of the town was the first to throw the torch into the synagogue.

Aschbach (Bamberg district)

BAROQUE SYNAGOGUE

The synagogue was completed in 1766 in a rural Baroque style. The Ark incorporated in the building is dated circa 1700. While the building was not put to the flames in 1938 (as were so many German synagogues) the structure was completely altered to accommodate residential use by private owners. A partial restoration was begun in 1987 when a cache of ritual objects was discovered under the roof.

Augsburg-Kriegshaber

JEWISH QUARTER

The synagogue is the focus of a Jewish quarter, mostly of the 17th and 18th centuries, occupying several streets, and a cemetery of 1627, with extensions from 1695 and 1727. The synagogue is connected to some of the other buildings by an underground system.

The synagogue is owned by the city. Its exterior was renovated in 1985, but its well-preserved interior is not used presently. After restoration it may serve the Augsburg Center of Jewish Music.

Bamberg

BAMBERG CATHEDRAL   Domplatz

There is a statue of the "Synagogue Defeated" on the right side of the central portal. Below this statue is a figure of a medieval Jew wearing a pionted hat.

Note: The "Synagogue Defeated" statue has been placed inside the cathedral. There are two additional "Synagogue Defeated" statues located in the cathedrals of Trier and Worms.

ANCIENT JEWISH QUARTER   1 Judenstrasse

The remnants of a 13th century synagogue are incorporated into the Turnhalle. It is located in the ancient Jewish quarter at 1 Judenstrasse. The Jews of Bamberg were driven from the city following the Black Plague of 1349.

Bayreuth

ANCIENT SYNAGOGUE   10 Grunewaldstrasse

This 17th century synagogue was destroyed by the Nazis during the war but has since been restored.

BERGEN-BELSEN CONCENTRATION CAMP SITE

The concentration camp was totally dismantled following the

war. The site of the camp is near the City of Bergen, which is about two hours from Hamburg on Autobahn A-7. There are several monuments and memorial stones dedicated to the memory of those who perished in this notorious death camp.

In the final months of the war, the camp population swelled, and the death rate soared, as prisoners from other death camps that had already fallen to the Allies were herded into Bergen-Belsen. Unlike the prototypical death camp, prisoners destined for Bergen-Belsen were let off the transports at a railroad platform four miles away and marched through a town to the camp.

In the last six weeks before the British liberated this camp (April 15, 1945), 36,000 inmates died, including a 16-year-old from Amsterdam, Anne Frank.

Berlin

CHECKPOINT CHARLIE (Former)

This was the site of the Berlin Wall. East Berlin was officially opened to all citizens of Germany on November 9, 1989, on the 51st anniversary of the *Kristallnacht.*

ORANIENBURGERSTRASSE SYNAGOGUE

30 Oranienbergerstrasse   Tel. 282-33-27

This synagogue was designed in 1859 by Eduard Knoblauch and August Stueler and was completed in 1866. It was designed in Moorish and Gothic forms and combined the use of polychrome brick and cast iron. This was the largest synagogue in Germany, with a seating capacity of 3,200. The greatest cantors of Europe officiated in this synagogue.

Adjoining the synagogue, on the right, is the present day Jewish Community Center. On the left, was a Jewish hospital and Jewish museum. On November 9, 1938, the Nazis set fire to the synagogue. The adjoining buildings at the time, housed German (non-Jewish) residents who persuaded the Gestapo to extinguish the fire in the synagogue since it would next burn down their homes. The Nazis did extinguish the fires, only after all of the interior of the synagogue was totally

Oranienburgerstrasse Temple is now being restored.

gutted. During the Allied bombing of the city, the synagogue was "hit" several times. To this day, the skeletal shell of the synagogue remains as a testament to the Nazi horrors. The former Communist government of East Berlin declared that it would restore the old Oranienburgerstrasse Synagogue to its original beauty. It is now being restored by the "unified" German government.

HOLCAUST MUSEUM
56-58 Am Grossen Wannsee
This villa was the site where Hitler and his officials assembled on January 20, 1942 to map plans for the implementation of the "final solution" - the extermination of European Jewry. The building was opened on January 20, 1992 as Berlin's first tribute honoring all those millions of Jewish victims killed during the Holocaust.

JEWISH COMMUNITY CENTER
80 Fasanenstrasse   Tel. 884-20-339
Located near the Kurfurstendam, the Jewish Community Center was built on the site of Berlin's most fashionable synagogue, the Fasanenstrasse Temple. The temple was built in 1912 by architect Ehrenfried Hessel in the Romanesque Revival style. Its dominant feature was its three-domed roof. The wedding chamber, in the basement, was decorated with tiles from the Imperial factory, a gift from the Kaiser, who had taken a personal interest in the building of the temple. The Fasanenstrasse Temple was totally destroyed during the Kristallnacht. All that remains is the front limestone portal,

which has been placed in sharp contrast, at the entrance of the new and modern community center.

The Jewish Community Center was designed in 1959 by D. Knoblauch and H. Heise. The community center houses a large auditorium which is used as a synagogue on the High Holy Days, a kosher restaurant, library, recreation rooms, and religious school. There are now armed guards stationed behind the bullet-proof glass at the reception area. There have been terrorist attacks against the community center several years ago. There are presently about 6,000 Jews living in West Berlin.

JOACHIMSTALERSTRASSE SYNAGOGUE

13 Joachimstalerstrasse   Tel. 88-42-030

This building houses the headquarters of the Jewish community, a library, kindergarten, kosher cafeteria, and reception hall.

PESTALOZZISTRASSE SYNAGOGUE

14 Pestalozzistrasse   Tel. 313-84-11

This synagogue survived the Holocaust, although it was severely damaged. It has been totally restored.

SPANDAU FORTRESS

This fortress was built in the 16th century. Part of the walls incorporate the tombstones from a 14th century Jewish cemetery which was razed in the 16th century. This fortress was used to house Nazi war criminals following World War II. The last Nazi war criminal, Rudolph Hess, died in Spandau in 1988.

BURNED SYNAGOGUE MEMORIAL

34 Munchenerstrasse

This was the site of a synagogue which was destroyed on November 9, 1938.

JEWISH CEMETERY

2 Lothringerstrasse   (in the Weissensea Section)

The *Judische Friedhof,* Jewish cemetery, is the newest and largest in Germany, containing more than 115,000 graves. The cemetery was restored and reconstructed after World War II. Among the black granite mausoleums, are the great personalities in German-Jewish history between 1880 and 1939.

The Orthodox section, known as the Adath Israel Cemetery, has not been restored. Many of the tombstones are still knocked-over, many are missing, and wild grass abounds. Funeral processions from West Berlinwere once stopped at Checkpoint Charlie. Only the hearse and non-Germans were permitted to enter into East Berlin before the "unification." The oldest Jewish cemetery in Berlin is located at 26 Grosse Hamburgstrasse.

Binswagen

SYNAGOGUE

The building is Germany's oldest extant synagogue in the Moorish style. It was built shortly after 1835. Its original windows and its roof survived the damages of 1938.

Buttenwiesen

SYNAGOGUE

The synagogue was built in 1856/57; the school building in 1846. The synagogue was restored in 1912. In 1938 the furnishings and the ritual objects of the synagogue were destroyed. What is now being restored is the Moorish façade. The mikvah of the congregation, the cemetery, and the Taharah Hall are still extant.

Cologne

ROONSTRASSE SYNAGOGUE

50 Roonstrasse   Tel. 23-56-26

Many of the synagogues in Germany at the turn of the century reflected the designs found in the great cathedrals of that country. The Roonstrasse Synagogue was built in 1899 by Emil Schreiterer in the Romanesque Revival style. The building was totally gutted on the Kristallnacht. It was not until 1957 when a small group of Holocaust survivors decided to rebuild. They commissioned Helmut Goldschmidt to redesign the existing structure. He divided the original hall of worship into two parts, horizontally, by putting in a floor at the gallery level. The domed part of the original structure thus became the main synagogue. Below the main synagogue is the social hall. The ground floor contains offices, a room for youth activities, a mikveh, daily chapel, Jewish Museum, and kosher restaurant.

Dusseldorf

HEINRICH HEINE'S BIRTHPLACE

53 Bolkerstrasse

There are several memorials throughout the City of Dusseldorf which have been dedicated to the famous Jewish writer, Heinrich Heine.

Ermreuth (Forchheim district)

SYNAGOGUE

The synagogue, a sandstone ashlar building of 1822, is being restored. It will house exhibitions and related events.

Essen

HOLOCAUST MUSEUM   29 Steelerstraase

The Great Synagogue in Essen was designed by Edmund Korner. He was inspired by descriptions of the courts of the Temple of Jerusalem which were closed by stoas. He designed the Essen Synagogue with a forecourt which was flanked by covered passageways. The architect intended that the worshipper should be moved by his subtle theatrical sense as he passed from the narrow entrance under the Neo-Romanesque façade, across the forecourt, and up the broader flight of steps through the spacious lobby and into the vast ever-broadening hall of worship.

The main sanctuary, which seated 1400 persons, was softly radiant with the light diffused through the stained-glass windows and reflected by glass mosaic tiles. Behind the Ark

The former synagogue in Essen is now a Holocaust Museum.

were arranged the weekday chapel, meeting hall, library, mikveh, offices, classrooms, and caretaker's and rabbi's living quarters.

On Kristallnacht, the Nazis attempted to dynamite the massive structure but found it too costly and structurally sound. The interior, however, was totally gutted. It has been restored following the war. The former main sanctuary now houses a Holocaust Museum. It is located three blocks from the main railway station.

ESSEN SYNAGOGUE

46 Sedanstrasse   Tel. 27-34-13

This concrete hemisphere, clad in copper on its exterior, was designed in 1959 by Knoblauch and Heise, the non-Jewish architects who designed the Jewish Community Center on Fasanenstrasse in West Berlin.

Frankfurt-am-Main

BORNEPLATZ SYNAGOGUE SITE

Bornestrasse is the present name for the street that used to be known as *Judengasse* or Jews' Street in the ancient ghetto. The synagogue on Borne Platz was destroyed in 1938. There is a marble memorial plaque attached to the wall of the old Jewish cemetery which is located behind the Blumen-Grosmarkhalle. The cemetery was opened in 1272 and closed in 1828. Entrance to the cemetery is through Dominikanerplatz.

JEWISH MUSEUM OF FRANKFURT

Untermainkai 14 (along the Main River) Tel. 212-50-00
There are 6,000 Jews in Frankfurt today. In the 16thcentury, Frankfurt was a major center of Jewish learning. Mayer Amschel Rothschild developed his money-changing business into Europe's leading banking empire. In the 19th century, Frankfort became a center for the Reform Movement. In 1851, the Orthodox countered this movement under the leadership of Rabbi Shimshon Raphael Hirsch. Before the Second World War, half of the Jewish community escaped to the United States and England. Many of those immigrants settled in the Washington Heights section of New York. Those who remained in Frankfurt were deported to the concentration camps. The majority of the present-day Jewish community came to Frankfurt from Poland and Russia following the war. The Jewish Museum of Frankfurt is housed in the Rothschild Palais, at Untermainkai, along the Main River. The exhibit

includes photographs, drawings, and Judaica from Frankfurt's Jewish history, dating from the Middle Ages to the Holocaust era.

FRANKFURT CATHEDRAL   Domplatz

The Jewish ghetto of Frankfurt was sacked in 1241. This cathedral was built during that period. Parts of the foundation of the cathedral contain Jewish tombstones. The Jews were expelled from the city during the Black Plague of 1348. The Jewish cemetery was again vandalized. This time, Jewish tombstones were used as part of the altar in the northern wing of the cathedral.

WESTEND SYNAGOGUE

Westendstrasse 43   Tel. 74-07-21

This synagogue was built by a Reform congregation. Following the war it was converted into an Orthodox synagogue. It was designed in 1910 by Franz Roeckle. It has a central plan and a domed hall. The Nazis had planned to establish a permanent museum to house Jewish religious treasures taken from destroyed Jewish communities throughout northern Europe. A similar plan was actually carried out in Prague, Czechoslavakia. The synagogue was therefore spared from destruction. The building was restored by the German government in 1950.There is a mikveh in this synagogue.

Friedberg

ANCIENT MIKVEH   20 Judengasse

This historic monument was built in 1260. It is located 75 feet below grade. The winding steps lead to a natural spring.

Gaukonigshofen (Wurzburg district)

SYNAGOGUE

The synagogue (dated 1890) was restored in 1988. It now houses a memorial to the Jewish communities of the region.

Georgensgmund (Roth district)

SYNAGOGUE & JEWISH CEMETERY

Restoration is in progress of the synagogue, built in 1734. The building also contains a mikveh. The work done so far has revealed a painted decoration presumed to have been done in the second half of the 18th century.

The cemetery of the community, dating to 1545, is being inventoried.

Hainsfurth

SYNAGOGUE

The synagogue was built about 1850. Its Ark, the original painted decorations of the door and the windows (the Ten Commandments) survive. A society of the Friends of the Synagogue is restoring the building. It will house a documentation center.

Hamburg

FORMER HAMBURG TEMPLE   120 Oberstrasse

The Oberstrasse Temple in Hamburg was designed by a team

of Jewish architects for a Reform congregation in 1931. Its design was stripped of older stylistic associations and was part of the new International Style practiced by such prominent architects as Le Corbusier and Mies van der Rohe. The building is now used by the German Radio Network.

HISTORIC EMIGRATION OFFICE
Holstenwall 24

Hamburg was the largest port of embarkation for European immigrants to America. Approximately five million passed through the city between 1850 and 1914. The man responsible for sending many of them was a native Jewish son of Hamburg, Albert Ballin. He turned his father's travel agency into the Hamburg-Amerika Line.

Visitors to the Historic Emigration Office can trace ancestors who passed through the port of Hamburg on their way to America. The museum has passenger lists of all ships that sailed from Hamburg from the mid-19th century until World War I. For a $30 fee, those who can provide a name and year of emigration will receive all the personal data (age, occupation, names of children, city of origin) of their ancestor. The museum is open Tuesday to Saturday, 10 a.m. to 1 p.m. and 2-5 p.m.

ALTONA JEWISH CEMETERY   Konigstrasse

This cemetery was established in the 16th century by Marranos from Holland and Portugal. The tombstones are lavishly sculpted with art symbols and Jewish emblems.

There is still is Sephardic presence in the city. Hamburg is the only city in Germany where Jews from Iran have settled in substantial numbers. The only Jewish hospital in the country, the Israelitisches Krankenhaus, is located in Hamburg.

The cradle of Reform Judaism was in Hamburg. Although some of the ideas took root in Berlin first, Hamburg is where the movement was organized and systematized. The first Reform congregation dates from 1818.

Hechingen

SYNAGOGUE MUSEUM   Goldschmiedsstrasse

This 17th century synagogue was restored following World War II. It is now a Jewish Museum. This street was formerly called Judengasse.

Hembsbach

RESTORED SYNAGOGUE

The synagogue located in the Rhein-Neckar district was built in 1845. It has recently been restored. The synagogue, a Neo-Romanesque building with high semi-circular windows and elaborate painted interior decoration, is now used for cultural events. The mikveh has also become a memorial.

Huttenheim (Kitzingen district)

During 1988/89 a careful inventory was taken of the synagogue (date 1820), the community center and the cantor's house next to it. Preliminary steps were taken towards conservation of the complex.

Ichenhausen

FORMER SYNAGOGUE

This town is located near the City of Ulm. The former synagogue was converted into a fire house following the war. The original frescoes with Judaic symbols are still on the ceilings. The former synagogue has recently been restored and is now a "Center of Encounter."

While in Ulm, be sure to see the magnificent Gothic cathedral. It has the tallest of all medieval spires - rising an unbelievable 630 feet. It is virtually a skyscraper.

Kippenheim

RESTORED SYNAGOGUE

The monumental Neo-Romanesque synagogue was built by G. J. Schneider in 1850. The vestibule has been turned into a memorial. The main sanctuary now serves as a restorers' workshop. Kippenheim is located in the Ortenau district.

Kitzingen

SYNAGOGUE

The synagogue, a monumental Neo-Romanesque building of 1833, is being restored. It will house a center for cultural activities; the foyer will serve as a memorial to the Jewish community of Kitzingen. Completion is expected for 1992.

Kleinheubach (Miltenberg district)

MIKVEH

The mikveh, a building of uncertain date, probably older than the synagogue which dates from the early 19th century, is being restored.

Kronach

SYNAGOGUE

The synagogue (built 1882) is going to be restored. Completion is expected in 1991. During 1933-45 the building served as a Red Cross station; in recent years as a storage space.

Landau

ANNE FRANK - HOUSE OF ENCOUNTER

Kaufhausgasse

This is the ancestral home of Anne Frank. This patrician home, built in 1602 , was purchased by Anne Frank's great-grandfather in 1870 for his fourteen children.

In 1987, over one hundred survivors of the Holocaust refurbished the house and dedicated it as a "House of Encounter." It contains an exhibition hall, restaurant, synagogue, Jewish library, Holocaust museum and conference rooms.

Mainz

ANCIENT JEWISH CEMETERY

85 Mombacherstrasse

Mainz was a center for Jewish learning. Such prominent scholars as Rabbenu Gershom ben Yehudah (*Me'or ha*

Golah), who died in 1028, Rabbi Klonymos ben Meshullam, and Rabbi Jacon ben Yakar, the teacher of Rashi, who died in 1064.

Rabbi Klonymos ben Meshullam was the first to institute the holy prayer, "*Unesaneh Tokef*," which is recited during Rosh Hashanah and Yom Kippur services. The author of that prayer was Rabbi Amnon who also lived in Mainz. The bishop ordered Rabbi Amnon to convert to Christianity. Rabbi Amnon said that he needed three days of grace to meditate upon the order. After he returned home he was distraught since he felt that he gave the impression that he actually might convert and betray his religion.

After three days of fasting and prayer, Rabbi Amnon refused to return to the bishop. He was arrested and brought to the bishop. He asked the bishop to cut out his tongue for saying that he "might" convert. The bishop did not cut out Rabbi Amnon's tongue but as punishment for not returning to the bishop and refusing to convert, all of Rabbi Amnon's fingers and hands, and toes and feet were amputated. Rabbi's Amnon's body was brought to the synagogue during the Rosh Hashanah service. Just before the *Keddushah,* he uttered the holy prayer, *Unesaneh Tokef,* and passed away. This prayer has now been incorporated into the High Holy Day liturgy.

Following the Black Plague of 1349, this Jewish cemetery was desecrated. The Jews of Mainz were expelled. The cemetery was restored recently. The tombstones are now numbered. No. 164 is the stone of Rabbenu Gershom ben Yehudah, No. 1 is the gravestone of Klonymos ben Meshullam, and No. 2 is the tombstone of Rabbi Jacob ben Yakar.

Michelstadt

ANCIENT SYNAGOGUE

This ancient synagogue was built in 1791 and has recently been restored. There is an ancient Jewish cemetery which contains the grave of the Baal Shem of Michelstadt.

Monchsdeggingen

The synagogue (of 1841) and the mikveh are being restored.

Munich

OLYMPIC STADIUM MEMORIAL

Connollystrasse 31

This is the site of the terrorist attack against the Israeli athletes during the 1972 Olympic Games.

DACHAU CONCENTRATION CAMP
(KZ-GEDANKSTAAT)

The first of Hitler's concentration camps was established in Dachau, a suburban town near Munich. This concentration camp was designed to house "political" prisoners, and was actually the prototype for all of Hitler's death camps. The original guard towers, electric barbed-wire fences, and moat are still extant. Some of the torture rooms have been converted into a museum, where there are preserved many articles used in daily life by the prisoners, torture instruments, and photographs of crematorium operations. The crematoria are located just to the left of the massive Jewish memorial and the "grave of thousands of unknown."

All of the prison barracks, except one, have been dismantled, but their site has been marked by concrete blocks and numbered gravel beds. It is estimated that 207,000 prisoners passed through Dachau, and some 27,000 are known to have been killed there. The original railroad tracks, which had a spur right through the center of the town of Dachau, have been torn up and have been replaced with a bike path.

How to get there...

If you are in Munich, take the subway, S-Bahn, from the main railway station. Get off at the station called "Dachau." Go downstairs, turn left and take the bus L-3 to Dachau Ost. Ask the driver to let you off at the KZ-Gedankstaat.

The Concentration Camp is open daily from 9:00 a.m. to 6:00 p.m.

Offenbach

FORMER SYNAGOGUE

The former Great Synagogue of Offenbach was built in the early 1900s. Its magnificent domed structure has been converted into a theater. The present synagogue is located just a few blocks away at 109 Kaiserstrasse.

Rothenburg

The Jews were driven from the city in 1298, 1348, and 1519. They were not permitted to return until the 19th century. The famed Rabbi Meir came from this city. (See Worms)

CITY MUSEUM

This museum has preserved many 13th century Jewish

tombstones. One stone contains an inscription referring to the burning of Jews in 1295 in the citadel just outside the town.

JUDENTANZHAUS (JEWISH DANCE HALL)

Judengasse

This timber-framed building of medieval design has recently been restored. It was in the heart of the old Jewish quarter. There is a low wall in front of this building which contains several ancient Jewish tombstones from the 13th century. The ancient synagogue was located on Georgengasse.

CORN EXCHANGE BUILDING

This building was built in the northern section of the city in 1588. There are several Jewish tombstones from the 13th century incorporated into the east and west façades of the building.

Schnaittach (Nurnberger Land)

SYNAGOGUE

The synagogue is now being restored. An inscription carved into its west façade testifies to its being built in 1570. It is a well-preserved ashlar building with a half-timber gable *(Fachwerkgiebel)*. The original doors and windows as well as the original vault are still in place. In the course of the present restoration two layers of frescoed inscriptions came to light.

The adjacent schoolhouse and cantor's apartment (17-18th

century) now house the museum of local history and culture
(Heimatmuseum).

Schopfloch

YIDDISH-SPEAKING TOWN

This small town, located about 100 miles south of Wurtzburg,
has a non-Jewish German population which speaks a dialect
of Yiddish! The dialect was known as *Lachoudish* (a
contraction of Lashon Hakodesh, Hebrew for "holy tongue").
Jewish residents developed this dialect, based largely on
Hebrew, so that their non-Jewish neighbors wouldn't
understand them. But over the years, as Christians worked in
Jewish homes and the Jewish community became well
integrated, everyone in Schopfloch learned the dialect.

The dialect contains some 2,000 words of Hebrew origin.
Water is "mayemm," a house is a "bayes," bread is "laechem,"
and the village itself is called the "medina." Instead of a
burgermeister (mayor), Schopfloch is presided over by a
"shofet."

Today, there are no Jews in this town. The former Hebrew
school is still extant. There is a memorial marker indicating
the site of the former synagogue which was destroyed in
1938. The old Jewish cemetery is still extant. The non-
Jewish German population still speaks Yiddish, complete
with the Hebrew words thrown in!

Schwabisch Hall

KECKENBURG MUSEUM

In the 17th century, there were itinerant artists who were commissioned to paint the walls and ceilings of wooden (*stahl* or barn-style) synagogues throughout Poland and Germany. The old wooden synagogues of Bechofen, Germany, was decorated by Eliezer Sussman, an itinerant artist from Poland. That synagogue was set ablaze during the Kristallnacht by the well-respected town-physician.

Other works by Eliezer Sussman have, fortunately, been preserved. The wall and ceiling paintings of the synagogue in the village of Unterlimpurg, where Jews had been expelled to, from the town of Schwabisch Hall, are now preserved in the Keckenburg Museum of Schwabisch Hall.

The interior of the synagogue room was commissioned in 1739. Eliezer Sussman used polychrome panels, depicting symbolic beasts in medallions against a floral background, as well as representations of Jerusalem and Hebrew texts. The women's section was behind a wooden screen with peepholes, which the artist contrived to incorporate in his decorative scheme.

The Keckenburg Museum is open daily (except Monday) from 9:00 a.m. to 12 noon and from 2:00 to 5:00 p.m.

Other works by Eliezer Sussman have been preserved and shipped to Israel. The remnants of a 13th century synagogue from Bamberg, which were incorporated into a church during the 1349 massacres, were recently shipped to the Israel Museum, in Jerusalem.

The exquisite wooden ceiling of the small synagogue at Horb, Germany, commissioned in 1739, is now on permanent

Ancient synagogue in Schwabisch Hall.

display in the Beit Hatefutsot, Museum of the Diaspora, in Tel Aviv University.

Speyer

ANCIENT MIKVEH   Judenbadgasse

This ancient mikveh was built in the 11th century. It is located just off the medieval Judengasse. There was an old synagogue within the courtyard. The key to the mikveh may be obtained at the nearby police station on Maximilianstrasse.

Urspringen (Main-Spessart district)

SYNAGOGUE

The synagogue, built in 1803, is a steep-roofed structure in the rural tradition. It will house a regional Jewish museum and memorial.

Veitshochheim (Wurzburg district)

SYNAGOGUE & GENIZA

The synagogue (dated before 1730) is being restored. Completion is expected for 1991. It will be rededicated as a synagogue, with a museum attatched which will house the *geniza* archives found under the roof of the synagogue in the course of restoration. This archive is of unique importance to the study of the history of German Jewry.

Weimar

BUCHENWALD CONCENTRATION CAMP SITE

Take Etterbergstrasse to the outskirts of the city and see the original concentration camp gate with its sign which says, *Jedem das Seine*, "To each what he deserves." The four concentration camp buildings that remain include: the crematorium with its six ovens; the main building; the former execution room, which now contains a museum of weapons of torture, lamp shades made from human skin and a scarf woven from human hair; and the prison laundry. 60,000 souls died in Buchenwald.

Worms

RASHI SYNAGOGUE

The original synagogue of Worms was built in 1034 on Judengasse. It was rebuilt in 1175, in the Gothic style. Later additions to the synagogue include a Frauenschul, women's section, in 1213, and the famous yeshiva, known as the Rashi Chapel, in 1624. Rashi, the noted rabbi who wrote commentaries on the Bible and the Talmud, was born in 1040, lived, worked and died in 1105 in the City of Troyes, France. He attended the rabbinical academy of Rabbenu Gershom in Worms only for a few years of his life, nevertheless, the City of Worms has adopted Rashi as its son. There is a Rashi House, Rashi Synagogue, and Rashi *Tor*, a gate along the ancient city walls.

There are several legends associated with Rashi's parents. A legend tells that his father cast a precious gem into the sea, rather than surrender it to Christians who desired it for idolatrous purposes. A heavenly voice then foretold the birth of a son who would enlighten the world with his wisdom.

The Rashi Shul was built in 1034.

Another legend tells of Rashi's mother being imperilled in a narrow street during her pregnancy. She pressed against a wall which formed a niche to rescue her. There is today a niche on the outside wall (in the alleyway), behind the Rashi Synagogue in Worms.

The Rashi Synagogue was totally destroyed during World War II. The present structure is a reconstruction, which was completed in 1961.

In the courtyard, behind the Rashi Chapel, is the original mikveh (ritual bath), which was built in 1186. It was not destroyed during the war. There is a natural spring which has supplied water for this mikveh since its original consecration. You can walk down the ancient winding stone stairs to the water level which is four levels below grade. Chassidim from all parts of the world come and immerse themselves in this holy mikveh before Rosh Hashanah.

Today, there are no Jews living in Worms. The Rashi Synagogue is now a museum and is open to the public. There are daily guided tours given by local Christian volunteers. They give out kippot or yarmulkas to all visitors to the synagogue.

RASHI TOR (GATE)

There are several protective gates along the medieval wall, which protected the City of Worms against invading forces. The massive doors have long been removed, but the names of each gate are still preserved with Gothic stone engravings. The Rashi Tor or gate is located at the junction of Judengasse and Karoligner Strasse. This was the entrance to the old

Jewish quarter.

ANCIENT JEWISH CEMETERY

This is the oldest Jewish cemetery in Europe. The earliest tombstone dates from the year 1076. Many noted rabbis are buried here. In 1286, when a great number of Jews wished to emigrate to Palestine, Rabbi Meir of Rothenburg (the Maharam) was taken prisoner. The emperor ordered this imprisonment because he hoped that imprisoning such a respected and prominent rabbi would prevent the Jews from emigrating. He did not want to lose a very reliable source of income, the so-called "Judensteur," a tax raised from Jews only. Rabbi Meir refused to let the Jewish community of Worms pay the 23,000 marks ransom for his release from prison. Rabbi Meir died in 1293 in Einshein prison. It was not until 14 years later that the ransom was paid and the remains of Rabbi Meir were released. A wealthy merchant, Alexander Solomon Wimpfen, paid the exorbitant ransom and was honored by being buried next to Rabbi Meir. Since the year 1307, the two of them have rested side by side. There are pebbles and slips of paper atop each tombstone. The little stones are symbolic of when the Jews buried their dead in the wilderness (after they left Egypt). In an effort to protect the remains from being disintered by wild animals, they heaped up stones on the graves. Today, the little stones are signs of reverence. The slips of paper have a similar significance. This custom is also observed at the Wailing Wall, in Jerusalem, where people put prayers on small slips of paper into the crevices in the Wall. It is a custom that the dead are buried facing Jerusalem. There is no explanation, but all of the thousands of tombstones (except one) in the Worms cemetery are facing south, instead east, southeast.

In the southern tip of the cemetery there is a small valley known as the "Rabbinthal" or "Valley of the Rabbis." Esteemed rabbis of Worms are buried here including: Rabbi Jacob ben Moses Moellin (Maharil), died 1427; Rabbi Elijah ben Moses Loanz (Ba'al Shem), died 1636; Rabbi Chaim Bacharach, died 1702; and Rabbi Menachem Mendel Rothschild, died 1732. Please note that Rashi is not buried in the Worms cemetery. He died in Troyes, France but his burial place is not known.

There is a wall along the north end of the cemetery which contains fragments of ancient tombstones. These are the remains of desecrated tombstones which were used to construct roads and houses during the massacres of the Black Plague in 1349.

The upper level of the cemetery is the recent section. The tombstones are engraved in both Hebrew and German, a sign of the assimilation process during the 19th and 20th centuries.

The Nazis did not touch this cemetery during the war. It was saved due to the efforts of the Chief Archivist of Worms, Dr. F.M. Illert, who showed the sites of Worms to the SS-leader, Himmler, when he was conducting a grand tour of the region. Himmler found the cemetery very interesting. When the Nazis decided to erect a warehouse on top of the cemetery, Dr. Illert argued that Himmler had a very special

The ancient Jewish cemetery in Worms is the oldest in Europe.

interest in the preservation of this Jewish cemetery. Illert recommended that the construction crew ask Berlin for permission before digging up the cemetery. Obviously, no one dared to make inquiries in Berlin concerning this matter. That way, Dr. Illert succeeded in blocking the plans of the Nazis. Moreover, he preserved the records and documents of the Jewish community, including the two volumes of the Worms *machzor*, dating from the 13th century. Much of this material has been sent to Israel.

Wurzburg

MAIN-FRANCONIA MUSEUM Marienberg Fortress This museum contains an ancient Ark from a medieval synagogue at Westheim. There are fragments of 14th century Jewish tombstones and paintings from an 18th century wooden synagogue.

KOSHER PROVISIONS

Bad Nauheim

Hotel Acadia   *Lindenstrasse 15   Tel. 3906*

Berlin

Community Center   *Fasanenstrasse 79   Tel. 884-20-339*

Schalom Snack Bar   *Wielandstrasse 43   Tel. 312-11-31*

(butcher)   *Eberswaderstrasse 20   Tel. 448-22-84*

Cologne   *Roonstrasse 50   Tel. 23-56-26*

Frankfurt-am-Main

Youth Center   *Savignystrasse 66   Tel. 75-23-41*

(deli) Aviv   *Hanauer Landstrasse 50   Tel. 43-15-39*

Heidelberg

College for Jewish Studies   *Theaterstrasse   Tel. 22576*

Munich   *Reichenbachstrasse 27/1   Tel. 201-45-65*

Stuttgart   *Hospitalstrasse 36   Tel. 29-56-65*

Wiesbaden   *Friedrichstrasse 33   Tel. 30-18-70*

SYNAGOGUES

Aachen   *Oppenhoffalee 50   Tel. 50-16-90*

Amberg   *Salzgasse 5   Tel. 13140*

Augsburg   *Halderstrasse 8   Tel. 51-79-85*

Bad Homburg   *Holderlinweg 28   Tel. 3740*

Bad Kreuznach   *Gymnasialstrasse 11   Tel. 26991*

Bad Nauheim   *Karlstrasse 34   Tel. 5605*

Baden-Baden   *Werderstrasse 2   Tel. 22142*

Bamberg   *Willy-Lessingstrasse 7   Tel. 23267*

Bayreuth   *Munzgasse 2   Tel. 65407*

Berlin

Dernbergstrasse 26   Tel. 321-20-56

Fasanenstrasse 79   Tel. 881-35-38

Frankelufer 10   Tel. 614-51-31

Joachinstaler Strasse 13   Tel. 881-30-31

Oranienburgerstrasse 28   Tel. (0372) 282-33-27

Pestalozzistrasse 14 (Liberal) Tel. 313-84-11

Rykestrasse 53   Tel. 448-52-98

Bielefeld   *Stapenhorstrasse 35   Tel. 12-37-52*

Bonn   *Templstrasse 2 Tel. 21-35-60*

Braunschweig   *Steinstrasse 4 Tel. 22417*

Bremen   *Schwachhauser Heerstrasse 117   Tel. 49-51-04*

Celle   *Brunkhorstrasse 48*

Coblenz   *Schlachthofstrasse 5   Tel. 42223*

Cologne   *Roonstrasse 50 Tel. 23-56-26*

Darmstadt   *Osannstrasse 11   Tel. 48719*

Detmold   *Allee 13   Tel. 22839*

Dortmund   *Prinz Friedrich Karlstrasse   Tel. 52-84-97*

Dresden   *20 Bautzenerstrasse   Tel. 55-491*

Fiedlerstrasse 3   Tel. 69 33 17

Dusseldorf   *Zeitenstrasse 50   Tel. 48-03-13*

Erfurt   *Euri-Gagarin-Ring   Tel. 2 49 64*

Essen   *Sedanstrasse 46   Tel. 27-34-13*

Frankfurt-am-Main

Baumweg 5   Tel. 29-46-92

Freherr-vom-Steinstrasse 30   Tel. 72-62-63

Roderberweg 29   Tel. 61-59-14

Freiburg   *Holbeinstrasse 25   Tel. 74223*

Fulda   *Buttlarstrasse 14b   Tel. 70252*

Furth   *Julienstrasse 2   Tel. 77-08-79*

Gelsenkirchen   *Von-der-Reckestrasse 9   Tel. 20-66-28*

Giessen   *Nordanlage 7   Tel. 31162*

Hagen   *Potthostrasse 16   Tel. 13262*

Halle/Salle   *Grosse Markerstrasse 13   Tel. 2 69 63*

Hamburg   *Hohe Weide 34   Tel. 49-29-04*

Hanover   *Haeckelstrasse 10   Tel. 81-27-62*

Heidelberg

Rohrbacherstrasse 13   Tel. 20820

College for Jewish Studies

Friedrichstrasse 9   Tel. 22576

Herford   *Riegelkamp 8b   Tel. 72739*

Lubeck   *St. Anne Straase 13   Tel. 76650*

Kaiserlautern   *Basteigasse 4   Tel. 69720*

Karlsruhe   *Kneilinger Allee 11   Tel. 72036*

Karl-Marx-Stadt (Chemnitz)

Stollbergerstrasse 28   Tel. 3 28 62

Kassel   *Bremerstrasse 9   Tel. 12960*

Krefeld   *Wiederstrasse 17b   Tel. 20648*

Leipzig   *Lohrstrasse 10   Tel. 29 10 28*

Magdeburg   *Groperstrasse 1A   Tel. 5 26 65*

Mainz   *Forsterstrasse 2   Tel. 63990*

Mannheim   *Maximilianstrasse 6   Tel. 441-295*

Marburg/Lahn   *Alter Kirchhainer Weg 1   Tel. 23228*

Minden   *Kampstrasse 6   Tel. 23437*

Monchengladbach-Rheydt

Albertusstrasse 54   Tel. 23879

Mulheim   *Kampstrasse 7   Tel. 35191*

Munich

Possarstrasse 15   Tel. 26-39-88

Reichenbachstrasse 27   Tel. 201-49-60

Schulstrasse 30

Georgenstrasse 71

Munster   *Klosterstrasse 6   Tel. 44909*

Neustadt   *Hauber Allee 13   Tel. 2652*

Nuremberg   *Wielandstrasse 6   Tel.33-18-88*

Offenbach   *Kaiserstrasse 109   Tel. 81-48-74*

Paderborn   *Pipinstrasse 32   Tel. 22596*

Passau   *Brunngasse 2*

Recklinghausen

Am Polizeiprasidium 3   Tel. 24525

Regensburg   *Am Brixener Hof 2   Tel. 56-26-00*

Saarbrucken   *Lortzingstrasse 8   Tel. 35152*

Schwerin/Mecklenburg   *Schlachterstrasse 3-5*

Straubing   *Wittlebacherstrasse 2   Tel. 1387*

Stuttgart   *Hospitalstrasse 36   Tel. 29-56-65*

Trier   *Kaiserstrasse 25   Tel. 41096*

Weiden   *Ringstrasse 17   Tel. 32794*

Wiesbaden   *Friedrichstrasse 33   Tel. 30-18-70*

Wuppertal   *Friedrich-Evret Strasse 73   Tel. 30-02-33*

Wurzburg   *Valentin-Beckerstrasse 11   Tel. 51190*

MIKVEHS

Frankfurt-am-Main   *Westendstrasse 43   Tel. 74-07-21*

Furth   *Blumenstrasse 31   Tel. 77-08-79*

Munich

Possartstrasse 15   Tel. 26-39-88

Reichenbachstrasse 27   Tel. 201-49-60

Wurzburg *Valentin-Beckerstrasse 11   Tel. 51190*

RAILROAD TIMETABLE

Munich to: Amsterdam............ 9:00 - 20:44

Berlin...................... 7:44 - 16:48

Copenhagen........... 9:30 - 22:50

London.................... 8:43 - 22:03

Paris....................... 7:19 - 16:59

Rome...................... 8:20 - 21:10

Venice.................... 9:44 - 15:36

Zurich.................... 9:08 - 13:50

GIBRALTAR

This fortified limestone promontory, known as the "Rock of Gibraltar," is situated off the southern tip of Spain. It is presently a British crown colony. Jews lived in Gibraltar in the 14th century when it was a Moorish city and became a temporary haven during their flight from the Inquisition of Spain. They later continued across the Mediterranean to the North African, Moslem countries, when Spain captured the Rock in 1462.

The present-day Jewish community dates from 1704, when England captured the Rock. During the Napoleonic wars, Aaron Nunez Cardozo was one of the foremost citizens of Gibraltar. His house on the Almeida subsequently became the City Hall.

In the middle of the 19th century, when the Rock was at the height of its importance as a British naval and military base, the Jewish community numbered about 2,000. Most of the retail trade was in their hands. During World War II, almost all of the civilian population, including the Jews, were evacuated to British territories, and not all returned.

Today, there are about 600 Jews, mostly of North African origin. Some are of English ancestry, some from Eastern Europe, and a few from Israel. There are four (Sephardic) synagogues which are all functioning. Many of the stores along Main Street are Jewish-owned. All of the Jewish shops are closed on the Sabbath. There is a Hebrew school, mikveh, and a kosher restaurant. The center of Gibraltar has an *eruv*. On the Sabbath and on all Jewish Festivals, the Israeli flag is raised above the Israeli embassy. Sir Joshua A. Hassan became the first Jewish mayor and Chief Minister of Gibraltar in 1964.

How to get there...

There are direct flights from London and Tel Aviv. to Gibraltar. The border between Spain and Gibraltar was officially opened in 1985. The nearest train terminal is at Algeciras, Spain. From there, take a taxi up to the border control.

There are ferries and hovercrafts departing from Algeciras to Tangiers, Morocco. From there you can catch another ferry to Gibraltar. Allow up to eight hours for the ferry rides. There are no direct ferries from Algeciras to Gibraltar.

JEWISH COMMUNITY CENTRE

7 Bomb House Lane   Tel. 743-12

Located around the corner from the Nefusot Yehudah Synagogue, the Jewish Community Centre houses a Hebrew school, mikveh, communal offices, and a kosher restaurant.

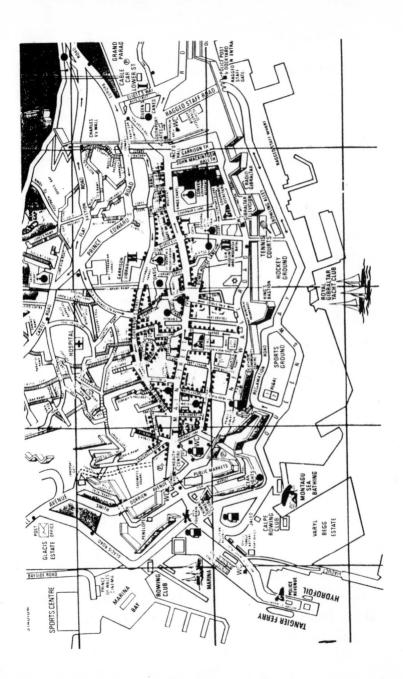

ETZ CHAIM SYNAGOGUE   91 Irishtown Lane

This is the oldest synagogue on the Rock. It was built in 1759 and is located upstairs, off a side-street entrance and has a seating capacity of about 100. It is almost like a *beit midrash* (small chapel), compared to the three other congregations in Gibraltar.

SHAAR HASHAMAYIM SYNAGOGUE

47 Engineer Lane

In this narrow street, the inconspicuous doorway leads into a beautiful Spanish-style courtyard. The congregation follows the Spanish and Portuguese (Sephardic) ritual. It was founded in 1748 and incorporates precious marbles and woods in its interior.

NEFUSOT YEHUDA SYNAGOGUE

66 Line Wall Road

This is the only free-standing synagogue on the Rock. It was organized in 1799 and built in 1890. There are daily services in the morning and evening.

ABUDARHAM SYNAGOGUE   Parliament Lane

This is the newest of the four synagogues in Gibraltar. It was built in 1820.

CITY HALL   McIntosh Square

Originally the home of Aaron Nunez Cardozo, a Jewish envoy and a friend of Lord Nelson. It is located at Linewall and McIntosh Square.

OLD JEWISH CEMETERY

Take the cable car up the Rock. Halfway up, stop and see the famous Gibraltar apes, which were brought by the Moors from North Africa. Continue on the cable car up to the top of the Rock. Walk to the right, towards St. Michael's Caves. St. Michael's Caves is a series of cavernous tunnels with spectacular stalagtite and stalagmite formations as well as an underground lake. It is rumored that the tunnels under the Rock of Gibraltar extend below the Mediterranean Sea, all the way to North Africa, about twenty miles away. St. Michael's Caves were used by the Allied Command during World War II as a bomb-proof hospital and air-raid shelter.

As you continue southward and downhill past St. Michael's Caves, you will pass the highest elevation on the Rock (1398 meters). Nearby is the Jew's Gate which is the entrance to the old Jewish cemetery. It contains the graves of many saintly men, including that of the revered Rabbi H.M. Benaim.

KOSHER PROVISIONS

Amar Bakery   *Linewall Road*
(one block from the Nefusot Yehuda Synagogue)
(butcher)   *McIntosh Square 26*

HOLLAND

The first Jewish communities in Holland were organized in the end of the 16th century by Marranos, secret Jews, fleeing the persecutions of the Inquisition of Spain and Portugal. Holland was then a Protestant country and offered the Jews religious freedom. The Jews encouraged trade and commerce. They introduced the diamond, tobacco and silk industries, opened sugar refineries, and played a key role in developing Holland's overseas commerce. They had mercantile and familial connections in Italy (Venice), India (Cochin), and helped organize the Dutch East Indies and Dutch West Indies Companies. The Dutch West Indies Company had branches in Brazil (Recife), Curaçao (Willemstad), and New Holland (New Amsterdam, which later became the City of New York).

The 17th century was Holland's "Golden Age." There were great accomplishments in literature, philosophy, and the arts. There were noted rabbis, scholars, poets, and scientists. Amsterdam was then known as the "New Jerusalem." The original Jewish settlers were Sephardic, but after 1630, there was a large influx of Ashkenazic Jews from Germany, Poland, and Lithuania. The great synagogues, Sephardic and Ashkenazic, were built during this "Golden Age."

In 1795, Napoleon ruled Holland, granted complete civil equality, which enabled the first country in Europe to elect Jews to its parliament.

In 1940, there were 140,000 Jews living in Holland. Although many Christians saved Jews by hiding them in secret attics, most of the Jews were deported and killed in the concentration camps. Today, there are about 30,000 Jews living in Holland. More than half live in Amsterdam.

Amsterdam

GREAT PORTUGUESE SYNAGOGUE

Mr. Visserplein 3   Tel. 24-53-51

The Sephardic community commissioned the master-builder, Elias Bouman, to design their *esnoga* (pronounced es-No-chah) or synagogue in 1671. The magnificent structure, completed in 1675, the congregation's second major synagogue on this site, was designed in the Classical idiom, best described as "Protestant Baroque."

The *esnoga* was built, as are all of the buildings of Amsterdam, on pilings above the canals. There is no cellar in the building. Four massive stone Ionic columns support the great wooden barrel-vaulted roof. These columns are symbolic of the four Matriarchs of the Jewish faith. There are twelve smaller wooden columns which support the women's galleries. These columns are symbolic of the twelve tribes of Israel.

Great Portuguese Synagogue of Amsterdam.

The Ark or *heychal* and reading platform, *teyvah*, are designed in jacaranda wood imported from the Dutch colony in Recife, Brazil.

During morning services, natural light floods the synagogue through the oversized clear-glass windows along all four walls. During the evening, since electricity has never been installed, the only source of light is candle-power. The *esnoga* is a breathtaking sight during the evening services. All of the magnificent brass candelabra as well as its brass candle tapers are aglow. There are six hundred and thirteen candles, symbolic of the 613 commandments of the Torah. Evening services are conducted in the main sanctuary only on the High Holy Days and on major Jewish Festivals. Other times, the small daily chapel, in the adjoining building, is used.

There is fine layer of sand strewn on the wooden floor planks of the *esnoga*. This is symbolic of the sands of the desert, through which the Jewish people wandered for forty years before entering the land of Israel. Another theory for the sand on the floor relates to the Spanish Inquisition. During that period, the Marranos or secret Jews appeared as Christians in public. In their homes, however, they practiced their Jewish faith. If they would be found practicing their religion, they would have been put to death. In order to muffle the sounds of their secret prayer services they poured sand onto the floor. This sand served as an acoustical muffler.

The courtyard in front of the *esnoga* consists of a row of one-story buildings. These row-houses contain the small chapel, which is used for daily and Sabbath evening services, a library, classrooms, the rabbi's and sexton's living quarters, and a mikveh. There is a 300-year-old *succah* in the courtyard. It was originally designed to be prefabricated, but do to its age and fragility, it has become a permanent structure. The small chapel with its panelled walls is like a room in a 17th century private home, except for the screened women's gallery behind and above the western wall. The Ark is a Dutch Baroque armoire of the period and is the work of a master cabinetmaker.

When there was a funeral in the 17th through 19th centuries, the body was taken below to the canal (since there is no cellar), put on a barge and rowed to the ancient Jewish cemetery in Ouderkerk.

Once a year, the rabbi, sexton, and an engineer went below the *esnoga* to inspect the structural supports of the building. Services at the Great Portuguese Synagogue follow the western Sephardic ritual. Men are seated downstairs and women upstairs. Services are very formal. The officials of the congregation wear top hats (cylinders). The sexton wears a long black coat and a bicorne, a cocked hat in the style of the Napoleonic era. The *chazan* or cantor also wears a long black coat, but wears a white cloth over his chest and a three-cornered round hat, similar to the attire of 17th century Calvanist clergymen. The *chazan* wears his prayer shawl (tallit) over his head. The service at the Great Portuguese Synagogue has not changed in over three hundred years. The tradition continues...

During World War II, before the Nazis entered Amsterdam, the Dutch authorities declared the Great Portuguese Synagogue a national monument. The Nazis had a policy of not destroying national monuments or museums in Amsterdam. The building was therefore spared from destruction. This was not the case, however, of the Great Ashkenazic Synagogue complex, just across the street from the Great Portuguese Synagogue.

The Spanish and Portuguese synagogues in London (Bevis Marks), Curaçao, St. Thomas (Virgin Islands), New York City, Philadelphia, and Newport, Rhode Island (Touro Synagogue) are all modelled after the mother *esnoga* in Amsterdam. Although the exteriors of these synagogues vary greatly, since they reflect the local architectural styles, the interiors are all designed with the Amsterdam *esnoga* as the prototype.

Note: Be prepared to go through a security check at the front gate of the *esnoga*. There have been attempts to bomb the Great Portuguese Synagogue. All handbags and cameras are stored in lockers at the front gate. Photography is strictly forbidden.

ASHKENAZIC SYNAGOGUE   Jacob Obrechtplein

Designed in 1928 by Harry Elte, the Ashkenazic Synagogue incorporates the International style of architecture. The design of this synagogue was influenced by the works of Frank Lloyd Wright. The gallery above the entrance to the main sanctuary rests on square posts which stand on a continuous pedestal. These short pillars are decorated with abstract, geometric patterns in the style of Piet Mondrian, the

Dutch painter who influenced modern design not only abroad, but also in his own country. Harry Elte, the architect and the cantor of the congregation, Landau, were deported in 1944.

Elte's treatment of the parabolic arch, which spans the niche of the Ark, is quite exciting. He divided the broad soffit of the arch into three glazed channels. Lit from behind, these sweeping curves of stained glass focus the worshipper's attention on the Ark, which occupies only a small area within the huge tympanum of the parabola.

The tall "steeple" on the synagogue's exterior, houses the water tower for the synagogue's mikveh. There are daily services in this synagogue.

OLD WEIGHING HOUSE

(Waaggebouw)   Nieuwmarkt

This towered building was originally built as part of the city wall in the 15th century. It was later used as a Weigh House, where ships' anchors and ordnance could be weighed. In 1690, the building was converted into a lecture hall where surgeons gave anatomy lessons. It was here that Rembrandt painted his famous Anatomy Lesson.

In 1975, the building was used as the Jewish Historical Museum. That museum was moved to the former Great Ashkenazic Synagogue complex at Jonas Daniel Meijerplein in 1987. There are now plans to renovated the Old Weigh House. Those plans include a theater and restaurant complex. The Nieumarkt was located just outside this Old Weigh House. It was originally a fish market, but in the 19th century, became a market for clothes traders. During World War II, this Nieumarkt was surrounded by barbed wire. Jews were gathered from their homes and assembled here before they were deported to the Nazi death camps.

OLD JEWISH QUARTER Rapenburgerstraat

The area around the Great Portuguese Synagogue, the Jewish Historical Museum, and the world-famous Amsterdam flea market was the heart of the old Jewish quarter.

WEST INDIES HOUSE Rapenburg ('s Gravenhekje)

This building was built in 1642 by the Dutch West Indies Company. It was designed as its warehouse. The Dutch West Indies Company traded with the New World colonies of Recife (Brazil), Willemstad (Curaçao), and New Amsterdam (today's New York City). Many of the shareholders in this company were Jewish. The company was organized in 1621 and disbanded in 1791.

FORMER GIRL'S ORPHANAGE
169-171 Rapenburgerstraat

This girl's orphanage was established in 1761 by the High German Jewish community. The girls were raised within an Orthodox environment. In 1943, the Nazis deported all of the inhabitants of this institution.

FORMER SYNAGOGUE Rapenburgerstraat 173

A progressive congregation used this synagogue from 1799 to 1808. It was later used by the Rabbinate of Amsterdam. The building was sacked by the Nazis during the war. There are still remnants of its religious functions in the Star of David set into the floor in the front entrance of the building.

FORMER NETHERLANDS ISRAELITE SEMINARY
Rapenburgerstraat 175-179

This was the site of the former rabbinical academy. Its most noted director was Dr. J.H. Dunner, who introduced many reforms in the training curriculum. The seminary was closed by the Nazis and was never reopened following the war. The building today houses offices.

ANDB BUILDING   Henri Polaklaan, near Parklaan

Henri Polak played an important role in the formation of the General Netherlands Diamondworkers Union (ANDB, one of the first trade unions in Holland). He was deported by the Nazis in 1943. The street has been named in his memory.

The ANDB building is the headquarters for this trade union. The massive brick structure was designed by the architect Berlage as a monument to the worker's movement. His inspiration for the design came from the "people's palaces" in Italy. The building can be visited during office hours.

FORMER PORTUGUESE-ISRAELITE HOSPITAL
Henri Polakaan

Located opposite the ANDB building, the Portuguese-Israelite Hospital was built in 1916. There is a stone plaque depicting the symbol of the Portuguese-Israelite community, a pelican feeding her young, on the front façade. This symbol also appears along the outer wall of the Great Portuguese Synagogue (on the Muiderstraat façade).

The hospital remained in use until 1943, when the Nazis deported all of the patients. Following the war, the society De Joodse Invalide took over the building. They have since moved and the building now houses the offices of Amsterdam's Communist Party.

PLANCIUS BUILDING   Plantage Kerklaan 61

Located across from the Zoo, the Plancius Building was established for a Jewish choral society. It contained a thousand-seat theater and a winter garden, complete with palm trees.. The theater was used as a synagogue on Jewish holidays. There is still a Star of David on the front façade.

Following the war, the building was converted into a garage and is used by the Amsterdam Police Department.

HOLLANDSE SCHOUWBURG

Plantage Middenlaan, near Plantage Kerklaan

This theater was located in the heart of the old Jewish quarter. Many Jewish plays were performed here. During World War II, the theater was renamed, Jewish Schouwburg. Jewish artists performed exclusively for a Jewish public.

It was in this very theater that the Nazis assembled the Jews of Amsterdam as an assembly-point, before they were deported. Their length of stay could vary between a few hours and several weeks. Following the war, the Hollandse Schouwburg Foundation bought the building and it was ultimately turned into a Holocaust memorial. The front façade of the building was completely restored. However, there is no theater once you pass through that façade. The ruins of the old walls, set in a garden , focus onto a simple basalt obelisk, rising in the form of a Star of David.

The Jews were marched to the railroad spur which was located just behind the Zoo (Artis), at Plantage Doklaan. They were loaded onto the trains and were taken to Westerbork.

DOCKWORKER MONUMENT

Jonas Daniel Meijerplein

Jonas Daniel Meijer was the first Jew to be admitted to the Bar in 1796. The street is named in honor of this great man who devoted his life to the emancipation of the Jews in Holland.

In February, 1941, there were mass arrests of Jews in Amsterdam. The dockworkers protested this action and held a general strike in the city. The communists called for this strike. All public transport also came to a halt. The strike was quickly broken by the Nazis by the use of force.

Every year, February 25th marks the anniversary of the dockworkers who resisted the Nazi occupation. The Monument of the Dockworker is located on the mall exactly between the Great Portuguese Synagogue and the Jewish Historical Museum. There is an additional Holocaust memorial in a small park, a few hundred feet to the left of the Jewish Historical Museum.

RESISTANCE MUSEUM & SYNAGOGUE

63 Lekstraat

This was the last synagogue to be built before World War II. It was designed by Abrahan Elzas in 1937 in the Bauhaus style.

This style of architecture is severe and lacks ornamentation. Following the war, the seven-hundred-seat main sanctuary was too large for its congregation. The congregation turned its main building into the Resistance Museum in 1985. The congregation still conducts daily services in its smaller chapel. The Lekstraat Synagogue has been declared a national monument.

JEWISH HISTORICAL MUSEUM

Jonas Daniel Meijerplein 2-4   Tel.   (020) 269-945

This was the site of the former High German or Ashkenaz synagogue in Amsterdam. The complex consists of two large and two small synagogues. The Great Shul (Grote Shul) dates from 1670. It was designed by the City Architect, Elias Bouwman, who also designed the Great Portuguese Synagogue across the road. At one time, the major road between the Portuguese and High German synagogues was a canal. The white marble Ark was donated in 1671 by Abraham ben Isaac Auerbach from Coesfeld. This synagogue now contains exhibitions but will be used for religious services in the future.

In 1686, the Obbene (Upper) Shul was established above the meat market which had been built behind the Great Shul. This little chapel was designed for the overflow crowds in the Great Shul. Another extension was required in 1700. The Dritt (Third) Shul was dedicated in a number of houses in front of the Obbene Shul in Nieuwe Amsetelstraat.

Finally, in 1730, the Neie (New) Shul was consecrated. This shul was replaced in 1752 by large new synagogue, which still can be seen today. Between the Great Shul and the New Shul was a mikveh and a complex which housed meeting rooms and the residence of the synagogue warden.

During World War II, the complex was sacked by the Nazis. Some of synagogues were used as stables and storage areas. In 1955, the abandoned synagogue complex was sold to the Amsterdam City Council. In 1987, the Jewish Historical Museum was completed and opened.

The Jewish Historical Museum is open daily, including Saturday from 11:00 a.m. to 5:00 p.m. There is no charge for Orthodox Jews who visit the museum on Saturday. (Note: There is an automatic door which is operated by an electronic impulse.) There is a dairy snack bar and a gift shop located in the former Obbene Shul.

MOSES AND AARON CHURCH   Mr. Visserplein

This church originated as a cladestine Catholic church (after the Protestant revolt). It is located directly across the road from the Great Portuguese Synagogue and the Jewish Historical Museum. There are large statues of Moses and Aaron above the front façade and miniature statues of the two holy men on the back façade.

It is believed that Baruch de Spinoza was born in 1632 in a house which stood on the site of the Moses and Aaron Church. Spinoza was the world-renowned philosopher who rejected the revelation, as laid down in the Torah, as a guiding line for human action, and replaced it by reason. In 1656, the rabbis of the Great Portuguese Congregation placed the 23-year-old Spinoza in *chayrem* or excommunication.

Spinoza retired to The Hague and worked as a lens polisher. When he died, his remains were not permitted to be buried in any Jewish cemetery. Recently, there has been a drive by the Liberal community in Amsterdam to remove the excommunication placed on Spinoza.

REMBRANDT'S HOUSE   4 Jodenbreestraat

Jodebreestraat was the business center of the Jewish quarter, where street trading as well as wholesale trading became established. Rembrandt lived in this house between 1639 and 1660. The influence of his Jewish environment can be found in Rembrandt's work. He was commissioned by Jews to paint their portrait, including Ephraim Bueno and Rabbi Menasseh ben Israel. Many times, Rembrandt employed Jewish models to pose for his sketches and paintings.

The building dates from 1607. In the 19th century, a Jewish merchant, Jochem Izak Aron Spitz, purchased the building. He was also a rabbi and turned part of this house into his synagogue. In 1906, the building was sold to the City of Amsterdam. Five years later, it was opened to the public as the Rembrandt House. This museum contains 245 etchings made by Rembrandt.

RIJKSMUSEUM (National Gallery)   Stadhouderskade

This is one of the world's great art galleries, containing nineteen of Rembrandt's paintings, including two of his most celebrated Jewish works, *Portait of Dr. Ephraim Bueno* and *The Jewish Bride*. Rembrandt lived and worked for seventeen years in the old Jewish section of Amsterdam.

Paintings which have Jewish themes or were painted by

Portrait of Rabbi Menasseh ben Israel by Rembrandt.

renowned Jewish artists such as Josef Israels, are located in the following rooms in the Rijksmuseum:

Room148: *Jewish Wedding,* by Jozef Israels.

Room 220: *Jeremiah Lamenting Destructionof Jerusalem,* by Rembrandt.

Room 221: *The Jewish Bride,* by Rembrandt.

Room 221A: *Portrait of Dr. Ephraim Bueno,* by Rembrandt, and *Interior of Great Portuguese Synagogue* , by Emmanuel de Witte.

The Rijksmuseum is open daily, including Saturday. A ticket to the museum may be purchased before the Sabbath, and left at the door, thereby permitting Orthodox Jews access to the museum, without violating the Sabbath.

ANNE FRANK HOUSE

263 Prinsengracht   Tel. 26-45-33

Many Dutch Christians hid Jews in secret rooms in old warehouses in Amsterdam during World War II. From July, 1942 to August, 1944, Anne Frank, a Jewish teenager, and her family went into hiding from the Nazis. It was in this secret attic, in the annex of a warehouse, where Anne Frank wrote her moving diary.

It was on August 1, 1944 that Anne Frank wrote her last entry in her diary. On August 4, 1944, a truck with German police and their Dutch cohorts, appeared at the door of the warehouse. They walked straight to the bookcase which concealed the entrance to the secret attic, shouted, "open up!" and siezed the terrified hideaways. A German policeman ordered everyone to hand over their jewelry and valuables. He took Mr. Frank's attache case, which contained Anne's notebooks, shook the contents out onto the floor and put in what he wanted to take with him. Anne's diary was left behind.

The hideaways were carried off, first to Westerbork and then to Auschwitz. All of the people who were hid in the attic perished in the camps except for Mr. Otto Frank, Anne's father. He returned to Amsterdam after the war and was given Anne's diary, which was found by the Christians who hid the Franks in the attic.

The Anne Frank House became a national museum in 1957. It is open daily from 9:00 a.m. to 5:00 p.m. For further information call 26-45-33.

GERARD DOUSTRAAT SYNAGOGUE

The synagogue located on Gerard Doustraat was built in 1892 in the Renaissance style . It was designed by architect E.M. Rood. Secret services were conducted in this synagogue during the Nazi occupation. The building was restored in 1969.

The Hague

SPINOZA HOUSE   72 Paviljoensgracht

Baruch Spinoza lived in this house during the last seven years of his life (1670-77). He earned his living as a lens grinder. This house is now a national landmark and contains a small Spinoza Museum.

SPINOZA TOMB

Following his excommunication from Amsterdam, Baruch Spinoza lived the remainder of his life in The Hague. After his death, his remains were not permitted to be buried in any Jewish cemetery. Spinoza is buried in the churchyard of the Nieuwe Kirk on Spuistraat.

FORMER SEPHARDIC SYNAGOGUE

103 Wagenstraat

This synagogue was built in 1726 by Sephardic Jews. It is no longer used as a Jewish house of worship. However, the building is a protected landmark. The Ark and holy objects were sent to Israel.

MADURODAM

This miniature Dutch village (scaled down to one-twentieth normal size) was assembled by the family of Captain George Maduro, who was a Dutch-Jewish hero during World War II. He died in a concentration camp during the war. This miniature Dutch village has a scale-model of the Great Portuguese Synagogue of Amsterdam. All revenues from this tourist attraction go to charity.

Ouderkerk

PORTUGUESE JEWISH CEMETERY

Located five miles south of Amsterdam in the village of Ouderkerk, along the Amstel River, is the oldest landmark of Dutch Jewry, the *bet chaim* or Jewish cemetery. The oldest tombstone is dated 1616. The unique and elaborately carved tombstones are fine examples of sepulchral art, reflecting a wide variety of biblical scenes and Baroque ornamentation. Some graves are simple, but many marble stones and monuments have exceptionally beautiful and artistic reliefs with poetic inscriptions describing the ability and excellence of the interred. The gravestones dating from the period 1650-1750 often depict people and angels, which is in opposition to Jewish precepts.

At the entrance to the cemetery stands the *Metaarhuis,* which served as the place for the ritual cleansing of the corpses. The Portuguese Jews spoke of the *Rodeamentos-House* or the *Huis der Ommegangen,* which refers to the practice of walking seven times around the coffin before the dead were buried.

There are many important personalities buried in this cemetery including; Rabbi Menasseh ben Israel, the distinguished scholar who pleaded with Oliver Cromwell for the readmission of the Jews to England; Dr. Ephraim Bueno, the physician whose portrait was painted and etched by Rembrandt and Jan Lievens; Don Samuel Palache, the envoy of the king of Morocco, whose funeral procession in The Hague was accompanied by the royal dignitaries such as Prince Maurice of Holland; and Abigail da Penha, the model of Rembrandt's famous painting, *The Jewish Bride.*

Baruch Spinoza is not buried in this cemetery, although his parent's graves are here. The Jewish community excommunicated Spinoza for his unorthodox philosophical views, which were believed to threaten the entire Jewish community.

How to get there...

Take the subway or Metro to Bijlmer station, then bus #175 to Ouderkerk. Look for a building covered with a thatched roof and walk toward the cathedral.

Note: The High German Jewish cemetery was established in Muiderberg in 1642.

Westerbork

This was the site of the World War II concentration camp, located outside of Amsterdam. It was here where over 110,000 Dutch Jews passed, on their way to the death camps in Germany and Poland.

Side Trips

If you wish to see twenty-five windmills in their natural setting, be sure to visit Kinderdijk. Take any train to Rotterdam. Then take the Metro or subway six stations to Suid Plain. Go downstairs to the bus depot and get a ticket to Kinderdijk (bus #154). It is about a 45-minute ride from the bus terminal.

The windmills were used in the early days, to pump water out from the sea and basically drain the sea and create new land. Each set of windmills was set on a higher level than the next. The windmills in Kinderdijk operate, in full sail, only on Saturdays.

KOSHER PROVISIONS

Amsterdam

Ha tikwa (Dairy)   *Kastelenstraat 80   Tel. (020) 642 42 99*

Mensa   *de Lairessestraat 13   Tel. 767-622*

(for students - open weekdays 5-7 p.m. only)

Sal Meyer   *Scheldestraat 45   Tel. 73-13-13*

Mouwes (deli) *Kastelenstraat 261   Tel. (020) 661 01 80*

Museum Café

Jonas Daniel Meijerplein 2-4   Tel. (020) 626 99 45

Theeboom (bakery)

Tweede Sweelinckstraat 5   Tel. 662-70-86

Maastraat 16   Tel. 662-48-27

Marcus (butcher) *Ferd. Bolsstraat 44   Tel. 71 98-81*

Mrs. B. Hertzberger   *Plantage Westermanlaan 9   (1018 DK)*

(Sabbath meals - reservations required)   Tel. 623-46-84

Delft   Hillel House   *Koornmarkt 9   Tel. 120-300*

The Hague

Mouwes (deli)   *Gedempte Gracht 85   Tel. 63-11-08*

Rotterdam

Piket (butcher)   *Walenburgweg 97   Tel. 467-28-56*

Utrecht

De Tarwebol (bakery)   *Zadelstraat 19   Tel. 314-887*

SYNAGOGUES

Almelo   *Molenkampspark 20   Tel. 2334*

Amersfoort   *Drieringensteeg 2   Tel. 726-204*

Amsterdam

Great Portuguese Synagogue

Mr. Visserplein 3   Tel. 24-53-51

Jacob Obrechtplein

Lekstraat 61

Gerard Doustraat 238

Linnaeusstraat 105

Nieuwe Kerkstraat 149

G.V.D. Veenstraat 26   (Kollel)

Buitenveldert van der Boechorststraat 26

Straat van Messina 10

(Liberal)   *Soetendorpstraat 8   Tel. 42-35-62*

Groenhof 79   Tel. 41-25-80

Arnhem   *Pastoorstraat 17A   Tel. 42-51-54*

Bussum   *Kromme Englaan 1A   Tel. 14882*

Deventer

Lange Bisschopstraat 19   Tel. 12594

(open for holidays only)

Dordrecht

Vrieseplein 17   Tel. 31817   (open for holidays only)

Eindhoven   *Casimirstraat 23   Tel. 51-12-53*

Enschede

Prinsestraat 16   Tel. 323-916

(Liberal)   *Tel. 324-369*

Groningen   *Folkingestraat 2   Tel. 123151*

Haarlem   *Kenaupark 7   Tel. 326-899*

The Hague (Den Haag)

Houtmaastr 11, Marsten Lookweg 44   Tel. 473201

 (Liberal)   *Prinsengracht 26   Tel. 656-893*

Hilversum   *Laanstraat 30   Tel. 13633*

Leeuwarden   *Sacramenstraat 19   Tel. 25123*

Leiden   *Levendaal 16   Tel. 12-57-93*

Maastricht   *Capucijnengang 2   Tel. 32320*

Middleburg

Nijverheidsweg 24   Tel. 13233   (open for holidays only)

Nijmegen

Gerard Noostraat 25   Tel. 23-19-38

(open for holidays only)

Rotterdam   *Davidsplein 4   Tel. 66-97-65*

Utrecht   *Springweg 164   Tel. 314-742*
Zwolle   *Schoutenstraat 14*

MIKVEHS

Amsterdam
Mr. Visserplein 3   Tel. 245-351
Heinzestraat 3   Tel.763-155
Haarlem   *Kenaupark 7   Tel. 242-051*
The Hague   *Houtmanstraat 11   Tel. 33705*
Rotterdam   *Davidsplein 4   Tel. 466-97-65*

RAILROAD TIMETABLE

Amsterdam to: Berlin.................. 7:44 - 17:04
Copenhagen....... 8:03 - 19:29
London............... 8:58 - 16:31
Nice..................... 7:00 - 22:49
Oslo..................... 8:03 - 9:04 (next day)
Paris.................... 7:00 - 13:00
Rome................... 8:58 - 7:58
Stockholm........... 8:03 - 8:47 (next day)
Vienna................. 6:59 - 21:25
Zurich................. 8:58 - 18:57

IRELAND

Jews have lived in Ireland for centuries. Following the expulsion from Spain in 1492, Jews arrived in Ireland, and settled in the port towns along the south coast. During the Napoleonic Wars in the 1800s, there was a new wave of immigrants arriving from Europe. The present community, however, stems from immigrants arriving from Lithuania and Russia between 1880 and 1910 following the pogroms.

There are former synagogues located in Limerick, Derry, and Waterford. There are historic Jewish cemeteries in Limerick, Cork, Dublin (Ballybough and Dolphin's Barn), and Belfast.

Some distinguished Jewish personalities in Irish Jewry include Robert Briscoe, the first Jewish member of the Irish House of Deputies (Dail) and the first Lord Mayor of Dublin, and Rabbi Isaac Herzog, the Chief Rabbi of the Irish Free State. His son, Chaim Herzog, is the President of the State of Israel.

Cork

CORK HEBREW CONGREGATION

10 South Terrace   Tel. 80-413 or 41-240

The Cork Hebrew Congregation was founded over one hundred years ago by Russian Jews. It is a very small congregation today, with only about fifteen members.

Dublin

DUBLIN HEBREW CONGREGATION

37 Adelaide Road   Tel. 761-734

This elagant brick Victorian synagogue was built in 1892. It is located in the old Jewish section of Dublin known as "Little Jerusalem."

IRISH JEWISH MUSEUM

Walworth Road (Portobello)   Tel. 780-822

The Irish Jewish Museum is housed in the hundred-year-old former Beth Hamedrash Hagadol Synagogue. The upper floor retains the original synagogue interior. The ground floor contains memorabilia of the Irish Jewish community. The museum's curator, Raphael Siev, is the only Jew in the Irish diplomatic service. The museum was dedicated in 1985 by President Chaim Herzog of Israel. The museum is open 11:00 a.m. to 3:30 p.m. on Sundays, Mondays, and Wednesdays.

OLD AGE HOME FOR THE HEBREWS

Leinster Road West   (Denmark Hill)   Tel. 972-004

The Ark and bimah in the Old Age Home were taken from the former synagogue on Ormond Quay on Dublin's River Liffey.

Limerick

In 1904, a local priest preached anti-Semitic rhetoric and instigated a pogrom. This was urged on by the merchants who were unhappy about Jewish competition. Jews were attacked and eventually left the city forever.

KOSHER PROVISIONS

Dublin

Bretzel   (bakery) *1A Lennox Street*

Erlich (butcher) *35 Lr. Clanbrassil Street*   *Tel. 751-865*

Fine   (grocery)   *84 Terenure Road North*   *Tel. 907-469*

Maccabi Sports Center (restaurant)

Kimmage Road West   *Tel. 504-938*

Movable Feasts   (kosher meals) *Tel. 562-464 or 943-947*

Mrs. Sharpe (kosher meals) *Tel. 900-550*

Mrs. Watson (kosher meals) *Tel. 933-549*

SYNAGOGUES

Belfast

Hebrew Congregation *49 Somerton Road*   *Tel. 777-974*

Cork

Hebrew Congregation

10 South Terrace   *Tel. 80-413 or 41-240*

Dublin

Hebrew Congregation   *Adelaide Road*   *Tel. 761-734*

Terenure Hebrew Congregation

Rathfarnham Road   *Tel. 973-218*

Machzikei Hadass

77 Terenure Roade North (rear)   *Tel. 908-413*

Old Age Home for the Hebrews

Leinster Road West (Denmark Hill)   *Tel. 972-004*

Progressive Congregation   *7 Leicester Avenue*

MIKVEH

Dublin   *Adelaide Road*   *Tel. 761-734*

ITALY

Italian Jewry is the oldest Jewish community of the European Diaspora. Its origins go back to 139 B.C.E., to the Roman Republic. From then on, Jewish connections with Italy and especially, with Rome, have been virtually uninterrupted to the present day. Large numbers of Jewish prisoners of war were brought to Rome after the destruction of the Temple in Jerusalem in the year 70. The Arch of Titus, in the ruins of the Roman Forum, commemorates this event with a bas relief showing the Jewish slaves carrying the spoils of the Temple; the *menorah*, the *shulchan*, and the silver trumpets.

There were large Jewish centers throughout southern Italy, especially in Sicily and Sardinia. Spain was in control of these regions and when King Ferdinand and Queen Isabella decreed the Inquisition in Spain, it applied to all of Spain's colonies. Over 100,000 Jews in Sicily were expelled in 1492. All of the ancient synagogues were converted into churches. The Jews then resettled in northern provinces of Italy and to north African countries.

The Jews of Italy were at the mercies of the popes. Edicts against Jews were issued periodically. Pope Innocent III, in the 13th century, ordered that all Jews must be distinguishable from Christians and decreed that men must wear a bright yellow circle on their outer garments and women must have two blue stripes on their shawls, similar to those worn by harlots. The Jews of Italy were later also required to wear a bright red velvet hat.

In 1516, the first ghetto in Italy was established, in Venice. The Jews were forced to live within a limited and enclosed space. They were permitted to work as moneylenders and deal in used clothing outside the ghetto walls during the day, but at sunset, all Jews were required to return. The last of the ghettos throughout Italy to be dismantled was in Rome, in 1870.

The Renaissance period of the 15th and 16th centuries was a cultural peak for Italian Jewry. Although they were still confined in ghettos, they prospered as physicians, scientists, and artists. They studied simultaneously rabbinical lore and the writings of classical antiquity, and taught the Bible and dancing, Hebrew grammar, and Italian poetry, all in complete harmony.

Some personalities of this period include: Leone de Modena (1571-1648) - rabbi, scholar, poet, and author of thirty-five books; Gershom Soncino - printer of Hebrew books around 1500; and Solomon ben Azariah de' Rossi (ca.1600) - known as the "Father of modern Jewish music," composer of Renaissance madrigal symphonies, and Jewish liturgical music.

On March 29, 1848, Carlo Alberto, King of Sardinia, extended civil rights to all Jews of Italy. Jews now entered every avenue of life in the new Italy. Some occupied high public office while many were distinguished writers, scholars, scientists, and jurists. During World War II, the Italians did not comply with the Nazis in "handing-over" the Jews. Most synagogues were not destroyed by the Nazis, however, in 1943, some 10,000 Italian Jews were deported to the Nazi death camps. Today, there are about 40,000 Jews living in Italy.

Ancona

GREAT SYNAGOGUE   Via Astagno   Tel. 202-638

There are two lavish 17th century synagogues contained within this building. The ground floor contains the Italian ritual synagogue. This is no longer used. The first floor contains the Levantine congregation.

The Piazza della Mostra was the site where twenty-five Spanish Jews refused to convert to Christianity, in 1556. They were hanged and burnt in this square. The other Jewish communities who had trade agreements with the port city of Ancona placed an embargo against the city for three years. It was removed after the Jews of Ancona asked the other Jewish merchants along the Italian coast not to hurt the economy of the city. The Jews of Ancona would be hurt even more if the embargo continued.

Bova Marina

ANCIENT SYNAGOGUE

While construction work was underway along the highway SS 106, between Reggio Calabria and Catanzaro, in the southwestern tip of Italy, a 3rd century synagogue ruin was discovered. The archaeologists discovered floor mosaics with Hebrew symbols. This is the second historic synagogue site in Italy, along with that of the 1st century synagogue ruins in Ostia Antica, near Rome.

Casale Monferrato

SYNAGOGUE & JEWISH MUSEUM

Vicolo Salomone Olper 44   Tel. 71807

Located midway between Turin and Milan, the Casale Monferrato synagogue was built in 1595. Its lavish decor contains a gilded Ark and wall decorations. The synagogue was restored in 1662, 1866, and after the Nazis devasted the structure, in 1969. There is a "Romeo and Juliet-style" balcony along the left wall. This was designed as the choir loft. The architects somehow forgot to build a staircase to this balcony. The choir therefore had to climb-up on a ladder to reach the choir loft.

The women's galleries and the Jewish Museum are located on the first floor of the building. This synagogue is only used on major Jewish Festivals since there are but a handful of Jews left in the city.

The synagogue in Casale Monferrato was built in 1595.

Cuneo

HISTORIC SYNAGOGUE   Via Mondovi 18

Most of the large cities and villages throughout Italy, at one time, instituted ghettos for their Jewish inhabitants. The synagoguein Cuneo, built in the 16th century, was located in the heart of the ghetto. In 1799, there were fierce battles in Cuneo between the troops of Napoleon and the Austrian armies. A bomb landed in the synagogue of Cuneo, near the rabbi's pulpit. That bomb has never exploded, to this day. It is still lodged in the wall! For information about visiting this ancient synagogue (at your own risk), contact the Cavaglion family at (60891) 2007.

Florence

GREAT SYNAGOGUE & JEWISH MUSEUM
Via L.C. Farini 4   Tel. 245-252

Started in 1874, its construction took eight years and it was inaugurated on October 10, 1882, after the official visit of the king of Italy, Victor Emanuel III. The synagogue was designed by the architectural firm of Treves, Falcini, and Micheli in the Moorish Revival style. The building underwent two major restorations. The first, following the Nazi retreat from the city. They placed mines beneath the pillars of the synagogue. An ax-mark still appears on one of the Ark doors, left by the Nazi stormtroopers. The second major restoration occurred after the terrible flood of 1966.

The congregation follows the Italian ritual. The interior walls and domed ceiling are finished in stenciled polychrome decorative patterns, typical of Moorish design. The plan of the synagogue is in the shape of a cross. The rabbi's pulpit is raised on a platform, reached by a winding stair. These Christian architectural forms were incorporated in this synagogue since two of the architects on the project were Christian.

On the synagogue grounds are communal buildings which house the Hebrew school and mikveh. There is a Holocaust

Great Synagogue of Florence.

memorial in the garden to the left of the synagogue.

The Jewish Museum is located on the third floor of the synagogue. There are several ritual artifacts as well as photographs and sketches of the old synagogue which was located in the ancient ghetto of Florence. The Arks from the ghetto synagogues were shipped to Israel (Yad Hagiborim Synagogue in Ramat Gan and to the Yeshiva Kerem be' Yavneh).

ANCIENT GHETTO

The Statue of David was designed by Michelangelo in 1504. The statue is housed in the Academia dell Belle Arti. A copy of the statue stands in the Piazza della Signori, near the site of the ancient ghetto of Florence. The ghetto was established in 1570 and was located in the infamous market quarter. The city architects redesigned the existing old buildings into one continuous structure which were entered through three portals. This one building block had a network of tightly woven passageways, arcades, and courtyards. All exterior windows were sealed-up.

The ghetto was dismantled in 1848, 278 years after it was established. The decaying buildings were demolished by the city as part of an urban renewal project. It was located between the present Piazza della Repubblica and Piazza dell'Olio. The only signs of the ghetto are the square and street names such as Via Condotta and Cortile de Bagne, the site of an ancient mikveh.

BASILICA OF ST. CROCE

This church was designed by architect Nicholo Matas, a Jew from Ancona. The Franciscan monks didn't realize that he was Jewish although his contract specified that no work be done on Saturdays. The front façade of the church contains a very prominent Star of David.

After the architect's death, he embarassed both the Jewish and Catholic communities of Florence. His contract with the church specified that, upon his death, he be buried in the basilica! This insult was resolved by placing his tomb under a ramp near the front stairs of the basilica.

Fossoli

CONCENTRATION CAMP MEMORIAL

During World War II, the Fossoli Concentration Camp was the site where the Italian Jews were assembled before they were deported to the death camps in Germany and Poland. Fossoli is located near the City of Carpi.

Livorno

In 1548, Cosimo I de Medici wanted to develop the cities of Livorno and Pisa into free trading ports. He issued an invitation to all people, promising amnesties, tax exemptions, and freedom of trade and religion. Ferdinand I de Medici extended the invitation further to the Jews of Europe by not compelling them to wear the yellow badges, to attend sermons, or to be forced into conversion. He permitted the construction of synagogues and granted Tuscan Jews

Great Synagogue of Livorno.

citizenship.

Thousands of Jews accepted this invitation, especially from Spain and Portugal, and created what was to be known as the "Jerusalem of Italy." Livorno never had a ghetto. The Jews lived in a quarter in the center of the city, free from all regulations. There was great cultural development. At one time there were six theological academies and schools for humanist studies. Sir Moses Montefiore was born in Livorno on October 24, 1874, while his parents were on a visit from England.

GREAT SYNAGOGUE

Piazza del Benamozeg   Tel. 24290

The Great Synagogue of Livorno was built in 1602 and was said to have been the finest in Italy. It was destroyed by Allied bombings during raids on the ports, during World War II.

The new synagogue was built in 1962 on the site of the original 1602 building. It is a modern structure, designed by architect Di Castro. The shape of the pre-cast concrete structure symbolizes the crown of the Torah. The interior is designed in an ellipse, with seating laid-out in a circular plan. The Ark was taken from the former17th century synagogue in Pesaro. Its Baroque design utilizes gilded floral patterns and a crown of the Torah.

The basement of the synagogue houses an Ark and bimah from the 17th century Spanish Synagogue of Ferrara. The Ark in the Oratory on Via Micali, which is gilded and capped with three quadrangular domes, is said to have been brought by Portuguese Jewish exiles who flooded into Livorno in the

15th century. The Jewish Community Center is located next to the synagogue.

Mantua

CHURCH OF THE MADONNA DELLA VICTORIA

In 1496, the wealthiest Jew in Mantua, Daniele Norsa, was accused of desecrating the image of the Madonna which was affixed to the exterior of his house. He was forced to demolish his house and, at his own expense, construct the Church of the Madonna della Victoria on the same site. There is a painting by an unknown artist (of the school of Mantegna) which depicts this incident. The Madonna is seen holding the new church which was named in her honor. At the bottom of the painting are portrayals of the Jews of Mantua, including Daniele Norsa. All of the Jews are wearing the special identification marks, the yellow badge, on their outer garments.

NORSA SYNAGOGUE   Via Govi 11   Tel. 321-490

This small chapel was designed by the wealthy Jewish merchant, Daniele Norsa. It was located in the heart of the ancient ghetto of Mantua. The lavish chapel is now only used on special occasions and on major Jewish Festivals.

Many of the former synagogues in Mantua have closed. Their Arks and reading platforms have been shipped to Israel or to other synagogues in Italy. Those sent to Israel are now housed in the Ponivez Yeshiva in B'nei Braq, the Beit Yeshayahu Synagogue in Tel Aviv, and in the Haychal Shlomo (Israel's Chief Rabbinate) in Jerusalem.

Ostia Antica

ANCIENT SYNAGOGUE

During the construction of the highway near Rome International Airport in 1961, the archaeological remains of a 3rd century synagogue (built upon a 1st century synagogue) in the ancient seaport of Ostia, were discovered. Two architraves, each with a sculptural *menorah, lulav, shofar,* and *etrog* were proof that this ancient ruin was originally a synagogue.

There was an entrance with three doors facing eastward, towards Jerusalem. There was a mikveh, an oven used for baking matzoh, and a small yeshiva.

How to get there...

Take the Rome Metro or subway towards Ostia. Get off at Ostia Antica, cross over the foot-bridge. The ancient synagogue is located at the far southern end of the archaeological park. The park is open daily (except Monday) from 10:00 a.m. to 5:00 p.m.

Pisa

LEANING TOWER OF PISA

The bell tower which was completed in the 14th century, was built on unstable soil. It rises about 80 feet and truly "leans" 14 feet off-center. Pisa was one of the "protected" cities. The Medicis invited Jews to Pisa and Livorno following the Inquisition in Spain and Portugal, in order to build up the economies of these two port cities. The Jews of Pisa were

Leaning Tower of Pisa.

never forced to live in a ghetto. The synagogue of Pisa is located at Via Palestro 24. The ancient Jewish cemetery is located within the vicinity of the Leaning Tower of Pisa. It is to the southwest of the Piazza of the Duomo. The Campo Santo is a mausoleum, a structure in which the Christians buried their dead (above ground). Just to the left of the Campo Santo is a wooden gate which leads to the ancient Jewish cemetery of Pisa.

Note: The Leaning Tower of Pisa was closed to all visitors in 1990 because of fear that it was structurally unsound.

Pompeii

Before the devastating eruption of Mount Vesuvius in the year 79, there was an active Jewish community in Pompeii. There are ruins of a Jewish-owned hotel, which had twenty-five rooms. The hotel ruins is located at Reg. VII, Section 12, Numbers 11-14.

Rome

ARCH OF TITUS

Built in the year 81 by Emperor Domitian, the Arch of Titus commemorates the destruction of the Temple of Jerusalem in the year 70 by Titus Vespasianus Augustus. There is a bas relief under the arch depicting Jewish slaves carrying the loot from the Temple, including the *menorah*, *shulchan*, and the silver trumpets. There was a very large existing Jewish community in Rome watching these Jewish slaves marching under the Arch of Titus. They collected monies to buy freedom for some of these Jewish slaves.

The Talmud placed a prohibition against Jews from walking under the Arch of Titus. During the Middle Ages, the elders of the Jewish community in Rome were permitted to leave their ghetto but were forced to carry their Torahs in a processional under the Arch of Titus and ridiculed by the local Christians. When the State of Israel was created in 1948, the Chief Rabbi of Rome granted the Jews permission to dance under the Arch of Titus in celebration of that historic event. The Arch of Titus is located at the beginning of the Via Sacra in the Roman Forum.

Jews slaves portrayed in the Arch of Titus.

THE COLOSSEUM

This great amphitheatre was begun by the Emperor Vespasian in the year 72 and completed by his son Titus in the year 80. Many Jewish slaves who were brought to Rome after the destruction of the Temple in Jerusalem, were used for the construction of the Colosseum.

MAMERTINE PRISON

Built in the 2nd century, the Mamertine Prison was used as a state prison and a place for capital executions. The prison is below grade. The prisoners were hurled into it through two holes in the ceiling. It was there that Aristobolus II, deposed king of Judea and , in the year 70, Shimon bar Giora, defender of the City of Jerusalem against the legions of Titus, were imprisoned.

TEMPLE OF DIVO GIULIO

This temple was erected on the spot where the body of Julius Caesar, in whom the Jews had found so much sympathy and support, had been cremated. The Roman historian Sventonius reports that, out of devotion, the Jews kept a vigil at Caesar's funeral pyre for a number of consecutive nights, and even half a century later, they still showed their grief before the mausoleum of Augustus.

ANCIENT GHETTO

The ghetto of Rome was established as an act against the Reformation by the Protestants against the Catholic church. The popes believed that the Jews were rebelling against the church as well. On July 12, 1555, Pope Paul IV established the ghetto in Rome. Located near the present-day Great Synagogue of Rome, the ghetto contained 130 tenement houses which were divided between two large and six small streets. The ghetto covered an area of one third of a square mile and housed 10,000 Jews.

There were three entrances to the ghetto which were locked-up at sunset. The Portico d'Ottavio is the last remaining ghetto gate. The popes closed down the eleven existing synagogues but later granted the Jews permission to construct only one synagogue structure. That structure housed five separate congregations. The ancient Arks, reading platforms, and Torahs are all that have survived. They are presently located within the Great Synagogue and its adjoining Jewish Museum.

The Church of Sant 'Angelo in Prescaria is located next to the Portico d'Ottavio. This church was just outside the ghetto walls. It was in this church where Jews were forced to attend the sermons and forced to convert to Christianity. There is a plaque on the façade of the church with an inscription written in Hebrew and Latin of Isaiah (LXV), where the Jews are reproached for their refusal to be converted.

The last ghetto in Italy, the Rome ghetto, was "liberated" in 1870.

JEWS' BRIDGE

The bridge near the Great Synagogue which crosses the Tiber River, the Ponte Quattro Capi (Bridge of the Four Heads), connected the sites of the oldest Jewish settlements of Rome.

The Jewish Hospital is located on the island, Isola Tiberina, in the center of the Tiber River.

On the other side of the Tiber, the building at 13 Via Dell'Atleta is said to have been a synagogue built by Nathan ben Yechiel (1035-1106), author of one of the compendia of Talmudic regulations called *Sefer Aruch.*

GREAT SYNAGOGUE

Lungotevere Cenci 9   Tel. 65-50-51

The Great Synagogue was built in 1904, after the demolition of the old ghetto building which housed the five congregations of Rome. It was designed by the architects Costa and Armanni in the Assyrian-Babylonian style. The congregation follows the Italian ritual, *nusach italki.* Along the eastern wall are three Arks. The two smaller Arks on either side of the main Ark were taken from the old ghetto synagogues. The Ark on the right side was taken from the former Sicilian Synagogue (Scola) and bears the date 1586. The Jews were expelled from Sicily in 1492, when Spain (who controlled Sicily at the time) issued its Inquisition decree.

The Ark from the Spanish Synagogue (Sculo) is located in the basement of the building. There are services conducted in the Spanish liturgy in that chapel.

In 1987, history was made when Pope John Paul II visited the Great Synagogue of Rome. This was the first papal visit to any synagogue in the history.

JEWISH MUSEUM OF ROME

Lungotevere Cenci 9   Tel. 65-64-648

Great Synagogue of Rome.

The Jewish Museum of Rome is located within the same building as the Great Synagogue. Some of the ancient items on display include: plaques from the catacombs of Via Portuense and from the ancient 3rd century synagogue at Ostia Antica, silver Torah ornaments, the actual Papal Bull issued in 1555 by Pope Paul IV *cum nimis absurdum,*" ordering the Jews to live in a ghetto, and a glorious gilded "Chair of Elijah," used during circumcisions, dating from the 16th century.

The museum is open Monday through Friday from 10:00 a.m. to 2:00 p.m. and on Sunday from 10:00 a.m. to 12 noon.

Note: Be prepared to undergo a thorough security check before entering the Great Synagogue and/or Jewish Museum. In 1982, there was a terrorist attack against this synagogue where a small Jewish child was killed.

MICHELANGELO'S MOSES

In the Church of St. Peter in Chains (San Pietro in Vicoli), stands the great sculpture of Moses. It was created in the 16th century and depicts Moses with horns emanating from his head, This was due to a misinterpretation of a verse in the Bible (Exodus 34:35), where the Hebrew word *keren,* is translated as "horn" instead of "ray of light." It is said that the Jews of Rome would flock out of the ghetto on Saturday afternoons and watch Michelangelo work on this sculpture.

THE VATICAN

St. Peter's contains a marble column which is said to have been taken from the Holy Temple in Jerusalem. The column is located on the right side of the "Pieta Chapel"of Michelangelo. It has been recorded by Benjamin of Tudela (the Jewish Marco Polo), that during his visit to Rome in the 12th century, the Jews of that city told him that on the eve of *Tish'a ba'Av,* the ninth day of the Hebrew month of Av, which commemorates the destruction of both Holy Temples in Jerusalem, that this sacred marble column in the Vatican, weeps. It was this spiral column which inspired Bernini to design the Baldachino of the High Altar in St. Peter's.

The ceiling of the Sistine Chapel was created by the famous artist Michelangelo, in 1512. Michelangelo depicts a series of biblical scenes: the separation of light from darkness, the creation of trees and plants, the creation of man, the creation of fire, the fall of man, the sacrifice of Noah, and the flood.

Sardinia/Alghero

TOWERS OF THE JEWS (la Torre degli ebrei)

These towers were built by the Jewish community of Alghero in 1360. They remain as historic landmarks of a once-thriving Jewish community. In 1492, the synagogue of Alghero was converted into the Church of Santa Croce.

Sicily

It has been said that there were over 100,000 Jews in Sicily in 1492. Sicily, Sardinia, and southern Italy were occupied by Spain. When King Ferdinand and Queen Isabella issued the Inquisition in 1492, it applied to all colonies of Spain. The Jews had four months to leave if they refused to convert to Christianity. The majority of the Jews left. Those who remained, converted to Christianity in public, but in the privacy of their homes, they practiced their Jewish faith. These secret Jews were known as conversos and Marranos. All of the ancient synagogues built by the Jews throughout Sicily and Sardinia were converted into churches. There is little that remains of the Jewish communities.

Siena

GREAT SYNAGOGUE   Via delle Scotte 14   Tel. 284-647

The Siena Synagogue was built in 1756. It has been said that the marble columns flanking the Ark were brought from Jerusalem. In 1796, Napoleon's troops dismantled the ghetto gates. However, in 1799, reactionary mobs drove Napoleon's troops from the city. The synagogue was sacked and the Ark doors still display ax-marks from this pogrom. Nineteen Jews were taken to the Piazza del Campo and burned at the stake.

Soragna

SYNAGOGUE & JEWISH MUSEUM
Via Cavour 43   Tel. 69104

This synagogue was built in the 18th century and replaces an even earlier Jewish house of worship. In 1982, the building was restored and is now a national landmark. The synagogue and Jewish Museum are located on the second floor. There are ancient Arks from former synagogues throughout Italy on display in the museum.

Trapani

There is still a Via Giudecca in this city. It has been said that the Palazzo della Giudecca was an ancient synagogue. There were major Jewish settlements in Palermo and Syracuse before the Inquisition.

Trent

ANCIENT SYNAGOGUE

Palazzo Salvatori   Via Manci

This was the city in which the Jews were accused of murdering a Christian child, Simon, in 1475, and using his blood for the baking of matzohs. Twelve Jews were tortured and then killed for this "crime." The remaining Jews in the city were expelled.

The rabbis of Italy placed a "chayrem," or excommunication against Trent - no Jew was ever permitted to live in this city or province. This ban was removed in 1965, when the Pope condemned the incident and removed the sainthood from Saint Simon, who was venerated as a saint following his murder. The cult of Saint Simon has now been abolished by the Vatican.

Above the entrance to the Palazzo Salvatori is a marble plaque depicting, very graphically, the ritual murder of Simon. The building is said to have been the ancient synagogue of Trent, but was converted into a Christian chapel following the murder of Simon and the expulsion of the Jews from the city.

Trieste

RISIERA SAN SABA DETENTION PRISON

This was the site of the infamous detention prison where 837 Jews from Trieste were imprisoned, tortured, and then deported to the death camps in Germany. The Risiera San Saba is located in the industrial quarter of the city. It is now a national memorial and contains the original cells and torture rooms. The crematorium was removed by the Nazis before they left the city. There is now a rose garden in its place.

GREAT SYNAGOGUE

Via San Francesco 19   Tel.768-171

Trieste had a ghetto for about one hundred years. In 1771, Empress Maria Teresa issued the Imperial Laws of Tolerance, which granted full and equal right for all Jews . The Jews of Trieste had close ties with their co-religionists in Vienna. Trieste was ruled by the Austro-Hungarian Empire. Many Jews went into politics and other professions which were , for centuries, restricted .

The Great Synagogue was a symbol of this Emancipation. The Jews of Trieste were wealthy and commissioned the best architects. The budget for this project was unlimited. The firm of Ruggiero Berlam and his son, Arduino, designed the massive Roman-style synagogue in 1912. This synagogue replaced the four other synagogues in the city. There are lavish stone carvings on the exterior and gold mosaic tiles on the interior.

Turin

MOLE ANTONELLIANA

Via Montebello and Via Giuseppi Verdi

Following the Emancipation, the Jews of Turin wanted to build the tallest synagogue in Italy. In 1863, they commissioned architect and engineer Alessandro Antonelli for the project. The community wanted a building which would seat 1500 as well as provide facilities for a school auditorium, mikveh, wedding halls, funeral rooms, and residential quarters for a rabbi and the caretaker.

The architect kept on building this structure higher, higher, and higher until, after fifteen years of construction and many cost-overruns, the steel frame reached an incredible 619 feet into the sky! This was one half the height of the Eiffel Tower of Paris. At this point, the Jewish community abandoned the project. All funds had been depleted.

The structure now became a monument to the architect. It was dubbed "Mole Antonelliana," the Tower of Antonelli. At its base the building followed a simplified classical motif. Its dome, however, suggests an Indian or possibly a Siamese design. It was to have two levels of galleries: the lower used by the women, the upper used for visitors who wished to look without disturbing the services or worshippers.

The unfinished structure was sold to the City of Turin. It is a national landmark and is presently used as a science museum. The exposed elevator shaft rises in the center of what was to be the main sanctuary. There is an observation deck from which you can see the old city of Turin as well as

The Mole Antonelliana was originally built as a synagogue.

the Italian and French Alps. Mont Blanc is about 100 miles from Turin.

GREAT SYNAGOGUE & JEWISH MUSEUM

Via Pia V #12   Tel. 658-585

Built in 1884 in the Moorish Revival style, the Great Synagogue was bombed during raids in World War II. It was restored following the war. The main sanctuary is only used for major Jewish Festivals. Other times, services are conducted in the cellar of the building. As you descend into the cellar, there is a magnificent vaulted brick chamber which was originally used as a storage area.

The space has been converted into a daily chapel. The gilded Ark and reading platform, *tevah*, were removed from the former 18th century synagogue in Chieri. The reading platform is an octagonal structure raised on two steps. An open canopy of scrolls crowns the eight spiralled columns. The concept of this tevah is basically that of the Baldachino, the imposing tabernacle by Bernini, which encloses the Altar of St. Peter's in Rome. It is said that the columns of the Holy Temple in Jerusalem were designed as spiral shafts. There is also a Jewish Museum located in this cellar area.

Note: It is possible to eat a kosher dinner in the adjoining Jewish Rest Home. Reservations should be made through the synagogue office.

There is a similar Ark and tevah in the old synagogue in Carmagnola. That synagogue has been closed for some time since there is no longer a Jewish community. In the 1950s and 1960s several ancient synagogue furnishings were shipped to Israel. In more recent times, the Italian government has initiated a project to help preserve and restore its national treasures. Many ancient synagogues are now in the process of being turned into national museums.

Venice

Jewish traders and merchants from Ashkenazic (German) lands were living in Venice as early as 1290. They lived on the island opposite San Marco, originally called Spinlunga but later known as Giudecca, "Island of the Jews." At one point, there were synagogues on Giudecca but it is said that they were demolished in the 18th century. The Jews were also involved in moneylending and created pawnbroker shops throughout the city. The Jews of Venice were not permitted to own houses or real estate and were required to wear a yellow badge and red velvet hat so that they would be distinguished from the Christian population.

In 1516, the first ghetto in the world was created. It did not expel the Jews from the city, rather, the edict gave the Jews in Venice ten days to move into the old abandonded munitions foundry. The word "foundry" in Italian is *geto*. Initially, there were seven hundred Jews living in the ghetto but, over the next hundred years, the population swelled to five thousand. They were forced to build tenements seven and eight stories high which were termed Venetian "skyscrapers," since all of the buildings in Venice were no taller than three stories.

During the day, the Jews could circulate freely in the city. At sunset, however, they all returned into the ghetto where, during the night, the guards, paid by the Jews themselves, watched over the entrances and the canals. There were patrol boats circling around the ghetto during the evening hours.

Although the Jews were confined to their ghetto, the 16th and 17th centuries were an age of cultural and artistic development and brought to prominence many outstanding scholars. Rabbi Leone de Modena, equally versed in religious studies and ordinary writers, was the author of many works and a popularizer of culture. Many non-Jewish scholars attended his lessons and sermons. Sara Copio Sullam, a gifted poetess, was admired for her beauty and culture, and known for her literary salon which was frequented by learned men and aristocrats.

It was not until Napoleon invaded Venice in 1797 that the gates of the ghetto were torn down. The Jews of Venice were then made free citizens.

VENICE GHETTO

How to get there...

As you leave the railroad station, go down the stairs and turn left. Walk along the Lista di Spagna until you reach the first canal. Cross over the bridge and immediately turn left. Walk along the canal for about three hundred feet (to the pier on the canal). Look for a small archway on the right with a yellow sign printed in Italian and Hebrew. This is the entrance to the Venice Ghetto.

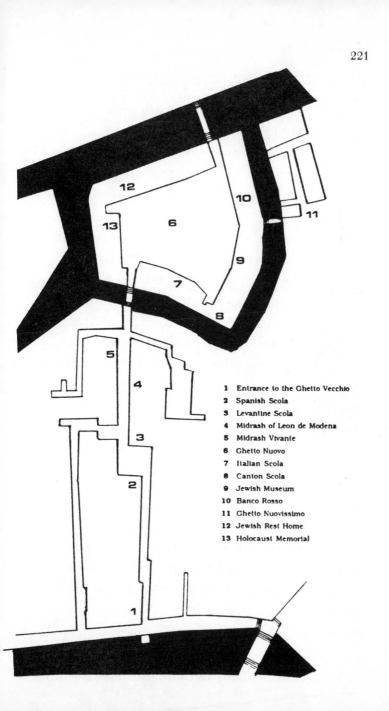

1 Entrance to the Ghetto Vecchio
2 Spanish Scola
3 Levantine Scola
4 Midrash of Leon de Modena
5 Midrash Vivante
6 Ghetto Nuovo
7 Italian Scola
8 Canton Scola
9 Jewish Museum
10 Banco Rosso
11 Ghetto Nuovissimo
12 Jewish Rest Home
13 Holocaust Memorial

CALLE DE GHETTO VECCHIO

The "old" ghetto (vecchio) refers to the second phase of enclosure. The Levantine Jewish traders were not forced into the original ghetto (nuovo) which was established in 1516. They were, however, forced into this area which adjoins the original ghetto, in 1541. The street name is called "calle" and not "via" since this section of the ghetto was dominated by Spanish Jews who fled from the Inquisition in 1492. The word for street in Italian is "via," and in Spanish it is "calle."

On the walls of this portico are still to be seen the signs of the gates which were closed at night, and the two small windows, now bricked up, from which the guards stood watch. There is a stone plaque beyond this portico, on the left wall, recalling the institution of the ghetto and listing all the limitations to which Jews had to submit and adding a note of the penalty for those who might violate these laws.

The building on the left, just beyond the portico, once housed a Talmud Torah (religious school) of the Ponentini.

SPANISH SYNAGOGUE (SCOLA)

The long alleyway leads into an open square (piazza), the Campiello delle Scuolo. The two great Jewish houses of worship, the Spanish and the Levantine Synagogues, are located in this piazza. In the center of the piazza is the well which was the only source of fresh water for the ghetto's inhabitants.

The Spanish Synagogue was built by Marrano (secret) Jews who fled from the Inquisition in Spain. They arrived in Venice, one of the few cities in Europe which allowed its

Jewish inhabitants to remain, albeit, confined within ghetto walls.

The Spanish Synagogue was built in 1554. The main sanctuary is located on the first floor of the structure. There was once a small Talmud Torah and daily chapel on the ground floor, just to the left of the vestibule. That sanctuary is in very poor condition and is not open to the public. The main sanctuary is an elongated space with the Ark along the eastern wall. The reading platform, *tevah,* is located on the opposite (western) wall. The seating runs parallel, along the north and south walls, respectively.

The synagogue underwent radical restoration in 1635, which tradition attributes to Baldassare Longhena, the great Venetian architect. The architectural style of the Spanish Synagogue is Classical-Baroque. Originally, the women were seated up in the galleries but in recent times, they are seated in the men's section, but separated by a partition. This is because the upper galleries have been found to be structurally unsound.

On Rosh Hashanah of 1848, Austria invaded Venice. Bombs landed in the ghetto and hit the Spanish Synagogue. There is a plaque along the *tevah* wall recalling this event.

The Spanish Synagogue is open for Sabbath services only during the summer season. During the cold seasons, the Levantine Synagogue, just across the piazza, is used. Services are conducted following the Orthodox (Sephardic) ritual. Men and women are seated separately.

LEVANTINE SYNAGOGUE (SCOLA)

Across the square from the Spanish Synagogue stands the Levantine Synagogue. It was founded in 1538 by the Levantine Jews. At the entrance hall is a plaque commemorating the visit of Sir Moses Montefiore in 1875. On the right side of the vestibule is a small study and prayer hall, the Luzzatto Scola. It was previously located in the Campio di Ghetto Nuovo (the original ghetto, established in 1516). Before its relocation to this building, the main entrance to the Levantine Synagogue was around the corner. That entrance is now closed-up. The Luzzatto Scola is not open to the public.

The main sanctuary is located upstairs, on the first floor. The plan of the synagogue is similar to the Spanish Synagogue. The magnificent reading platform, *tevah*, was designed in the late Baroque style and is the work of Andrea Brustolon, the noted Venetian wood sculptor. There are two wide curving stairways of twelve steps, decorated by columns that outline it effectively. The pulpit appears framed by two heavily decorated twisted columns, which recall those of Solomon's Temple in Jerusalem.

This synagogue is used on Sabbaths and Festivals during the winter season.

CALLE DEL FORNO

Leaving the Levantine Synagogue, one walks into a small open space, Corte Scalamata. "Scalamata" refers to the family which lived in this courtyard. Others say the "scalamata" refers to the steep and winding staircases in the seven and eight-story Venetian "skyscrapers." Turn left into Calle del Forno. This is the site of the small matzoh factory which is still in operation.

MIDRASH OF LEONE DE MODENA

Leaving the Levantine Synagogue, turn right and walk along Ghetto Vecchio. Number 1222 was the study (midrash) of the noted scholar, Leone de Modena. On the opposite side of the street was the Midrash Vivante, which was founded in 1853.

GHETTO NUOVO

Cross over the bridge and you will arrive in the site of the new foundry, the Ghetto Nuovo. This was the first location in which the German and Italian Jews were confined in 1516. The main square had three wells which served the original seven hundred ghetto inhabitants.

Jewish wedding in Venice, circa 1700.

ITALIAN SYNAGOGUE (SCOLA)

This was the last synagogue built in the ghetto. It was constructed in 1575 by the Jews belonging to the Italian ritual. It was the site where the great spiritual leader, Leone de Modena, delivered his famous sermons. The building is no longer in use. You can identify the building, which seems to blend in with the adjoining structures, by looking for five large windows with a crest above the central window. There is a Baroque umbrella dome on a high polyganol drum, from which the windows illuminate the *tevah* below.

CANTON SYNAGOGUE (SCOLA)

This synagogue takes its name from the Canton family, the rich German bankers who built it as their private oratory of the Ashkenazic rite. Others say that is was organized by Jews who fled from France (*le canton des Juifs*). It was built in 1531, but is no longer in use. It is recognized by its high wooden umbrella dome rising on an octagonal drum.

GREAT GERMAN SYNAGOGUE (SCOLA)

This was the first synagogue built in the ghetto. It was the German Jews who built it in 1528 for the practice of the Ashkenazic rite. The builder found it difficult to insert the plan of the synagogue in the pre-existing building, so its plan appears slightly assymetrical, almost trapezoidal. According to *halachah*, Jewish law, the synagogue must be the tallest structure in the city, conditions permitting. Since they were not permitted to build free-standing synagogues in the ghetto, they designed their synagogue in the uppermost level of the

The Rialto Bridge in Venice.

tenement building.

Originally, the reading platform, *bimah*, was located in the center of the space. The congregation found that they could accommodate more people if they placed the *bimah* in the back of the synagogue, along the western wall. All of the other synagogues in the ghetto later followed this design. When this synagogue was built, Jews were not craftsmen or artisans. They employed non-Jews for the construction of their synagogues. It was not permitted for Jews to incorporate any marble in their synagogues since this material was used in the Catholic church. Instead of real marble, they "marbleized" the wooden wall panels. In later years, this restriction against the use of marble was removed. Real marble is now found in all of the ancient synagogues of the ghetto.

The exterior of the German Synagogue is recognized by its

five windows, of which three are walled-up, with arches in white stone. The main features in this synagogue are the magnificent gilded Ark and bimah and the elliptical women's gallery. This synagogue is no longer in use. It is located above the Museum of Jewish Art.

MUSEUM OF JEWISH ART

Housed in rooms below the Great German Synagogue, the Museum of Jewish Art was created after World War II. Some items of interest are ancient mantles for Torahs, Ark covers, silver Torah crowns, a canopy (chupah) for Jewish weddings, and a chair of the prophet Elijah, used for circumcisions.

There is a project in the works which will create a typical living quarter in the ghetto. The ghetto had a network of passages which connected all of the buildings with the synagogues and meeting rooms. This was done in order to protect the Jews from ever stepping outside in case of attacks against the ghetto. When the ghetto was established, all windows which faced outside the ghetto walls were required to be bricked- up.

Tours of the synagogues in the ghetto are given daily, except on Saturdays and Jewish Festivals. They meet in front of the Museum of Jewish Art.

JEWISH REST HOME

There is a small chapel in the Jewish Rest Home which houses a 17th century Ark from the Mesullanim Scola, an Ashkenazic or German rite congregation which was demolished on this site in the 19th century. This chapel is used for daily prayers.

Arrangements can be made in the Jewish Rest Home to have an kosher lunch, on weekdays and on the Sabbath. Unfortunately, no other meals are available. For reservations, call 716-002.

HOLOCAUST MEMORIAL

On the wall adjoining the Jewish Rest Home are seven bronze memorial plaques commemorating the six million Jewish men, women, and children who perished during World War II. The sculptural plaques were designed by A. Blatas. There are similar Holocaust memorial plaques, designed by the same artist, in Paris and in New York City (in Dag Hammarskjold Park, on 47th Street, near Second Avenue). The original barbed wires, put up by the Nazis, are still visible above the wall of this Holocaust Memorial. The door to the right of the plaques is the ghetto mortuary.

During World War II, eight thousand Italian Jews were deported, two hundred were taken from Venice.

GHETTO NUOVISSIMO

Before leaving the Ghetto Nuovo from the other entrance point, look to the left. There is a door with a sign above which reads, "Banco Rosso." This was one of the Jewish pawnbroker shops or banks. Many Jews in the ghetto were moneylenders. Cross over the old wooden bridge and you will arrive in the Ghetto Nuovissimo. This was the "newest" ghetto which was added in 1633. It was built for the wealthy Jews in the city. There were no synagogues or shops in this section. Some of the buildings still display the Jewish family crests over the doors. This part of the ghetto did not have any Venetian "skyscrapers" or tenements.

JEWISH CEMETERY

There is no cemetery within the ghetto walls. Land was acquired in 1386 on the island called "Lido." At the Riviera San Nicolo 2, at the corner of Via Cipro, is the ancient Jewish cemetery. Some personalities buried in the "Cimitero Ebraico" include Leone de Modena, Sara Copio Sullam, and Daniel Rodriguez. Some of the ancient tombstones portray sculptural motifs, similar to those found in the ancient Jewish cemetries in Amsterdam and Curaçao.

KOSHER PROVISIONS

Bologna Eshel Israel *Via Gombruti 9* *Tel. 340-936*
Ferrara (butcher) *Via Saraceno 106a* *Tel. 33-996*
Florence
 il Cuscussu *Via Farini 2a* *Tel. 241-890*
(butcher) *Via del Macci 106* *Tel. 666-534*
Genoa (butcher) *Corso Torino 2r* *Tel.587-658*
Livorno (butcher) *Mercato Centrale* *Tel. 39-474*
Milan
(restaurant) *Via Leone XIII #1* *Tel. 496-331*
Mensa *Via Cellini 2* *Tel. 708-877*
Eshel Israel *Via Benvenuto Cellini 2* *Tel. 708-877*
(butcher) *Via Cesare de Sesto 7* *Tel. 83-51-011*
(grocery) *Via della Braida 2* *Tel. 588-248*

(bakery) Elli   *Via Radaelli   Tel. 474-427*

Milano-Marittima (near Ravenna)

Hotel Liberty   *Traversa 14   Tel. (0544) 991-281*

Modena   (grocery)   *Macelleria Duomo*
stand #25, Mercato Coperto

Rimini   Grand Hotel   *Tel. (0541) 24211*

Rome

Da Lisa Restaurant   *Via Foscolo 16-18   Tel. 730-027*

(Lubavitch)   *Via Lorenzo il Magnifico   Tel. 424-6962*

(grocery) *Via Portico d'Ottavia 1b   Tel. 65-41-364*

(butcher)   *Via Urbana 117   Tel. 487-743*

Pensione Carmel   *Via Mameli 11   Tel 580-9921*

Turin

(Jewish Rest Home)   *Via Pio V #12   Tel. 65-08-332*

(butcher) *Via Secondo 73   Tel. 50-23-28*

Venice

(Jewish Rest Home)   Ghetto Nuovo   *Tel. 716-002*
(lunch only)

Viareggio

(butcher)   *Piazza del Mercato Nuovo   Tel. 42-691*
(summer only)

SYNAGOGUES

Alessandria   *Via Milano 5   Tel. 62224*

Ancona   *Via Astagno 12 Tel. 202-638*

Asti   *Via Ottolenghi 8   Tel. 53281*

Bologna   *Via De' Gombruti 9 Tel. 232-066*

Casale Monferrato   *Vicolo Salomone Olper 44   Tel. 71807*

Ferrara   *Via Mazzini 95   Tel. 47004*

Florence   *Via L.C. Farini 4   Tel. 245-252*

Genoa   *Via Bertora 6   Tel. 891-513*

Gorizia   *Via Ascoli 13*

Livorno   *Piazza Benamozegh 1   Tel. 24290*

Mantua   *Via Govi 11   Tel. 321-490*

Merano   *Via Schiller 14   Tel. 34-999*

Mestre   *Via Borsi 28*

Milan

Tempio Centrale   *Via Guastalla 19   Tel. 791-851*

Ohel Jaakov   *Via Cellini 2   Tel. 708-877*

Beth Shlomo   *Corso di Porta Romana 3*

Oratorio di Via Jommelli 18   *Tel.236-504*

Oratorio della Scuola   *Via Sally Mayer 4*

Oratorio Sfardita   *Via delle Tuberose 14   Tel. 41-51-660*

Oratorio di Via Eupili 8

Oratorio Nuovo Residenza per Anziana   *Via Leone XII #1*

Modena   *Piazza Mazzini 26   Tel. 223-978*

Naples   *Via Cappella Vecchia 31   Tel. 416-386*

Padua   *Via San Martino e Solferino 9   Tel. 23524*

Parma   *Vicolo Cervi 4   Tel. 774-823*

Pisa   *Via Palestro 24   Tel. 27269*

Rome

Tempio Magiore   *Lungotevere Cenci 9   Tel. 65-64-648*

Tempio Spagnola   *Via Catalana   Tel. 65-64-648*

Oratorio di Castro   *Via Balbo 33   Tel. 47-59-881*

Via della Borgata della Magliana   Tel. 52-32-634

Temple Beth El   *Via Padova 92   Tel. 426-160*

Lungotevere Sanzio 12

Via Garefagnana 4   Tel. 42-44-521

Siena   *Via delle Scotte 14   Tel. 284-647*

Soragna   *Via Cavour 43   Tel. 69104*

Turin   *Via Pio V #12   Tel. 65-85-85*

Trieste   *Via San Francesco 19   Tel. 768-171*

Venice   *Ghetto Vecchio 1188a   Tel. 715-912*

Vercelli   *Via Foa 70   Tel. 66793*

Verona   *Via Portici 3   Tel. 21112*

Viareggio   *Via Oleandri*

MIKVEHS

Ancona   *Via Astagno   Tel. 55654*

Bologna   *Via Gombruti 9   Tel. 232-066*

Ferrara   *Via Saraceno 106/a & Via Carmelino   Tel. 33996*

Florence   *Via L.C. Farini 4   Tel. 210-763*

Milan   *Via Guastalla 19   Tel. 808-947*

Rome   *Lungotevere Cenci & Via Balbo 33   Tel. 65-64-648*

Venice   (Jewish Rest Home)

Ghetto Nuovo 2874   Tel. 716-002

RAILROAD TIMETABLE

Milan to:

Amsterdam	7:10 - 22:28
Athens	13:05 - 8:00 (two days later)
Barcelona	6:40 - 21:21
Brussels	17:55 - 7:37
Copenhagen	9:20 - 6:45
Frankfurt	7:10 - 16:17
London	19:05 - 13:37
Nice	13:10 - 19:18
Paris	8:52 - 16:23
Rome	13:00 20:07
Venice	9:05 -12:24
Vienna	9:35 - 22:20
Zurich	9:10 - 13:50

LUXEMBOURG

There was a Jewish settlement in Luxembourg as early as the 13th century. It was not until after the French Revolution that the first permanent Jewish community was established in 1808. During World War II, the Jewish community was virtually wiped out. There are today about 1,200 Jews living in Luxembourg.

Luxembourg City

ANCIENT SYNAGOGUE SITE   30 rue des Juifs

This was the site of Luxembourg's first synagogue. It was destroyed by angry mobs during the Black Plague in 1349. Relics from this ancient synagogue are preserved in the Judaica Section of the Alsace Museum.

GREAT SYNAGOGUE

45 rue Monterey   Tel. 27261

The former Moorish-Byzantine synagogue located on this site was built in 1894. It was destroyed by the Nazis during the last war. The present structure was built in 1953 and is located across from Radio Luxembourg.

Mondorf-les-Bains

FORMER SYNAGOGUE   rue du Moulin

This synagogue was not destroyed during the last war. It was used until recently only during the summer season by Jewish vacationers who were guests at the nearby kosher Hotel Bristol. That hotel closed down in 1987.

RAILROAD TIMETABLE

Luxembourg to:

Amsterdam	8:31 - 14:08
Copenhagen	7:00 - 20:45
Frankfurt	9:39 - 13:12
London	12:06 - 19:34
Milan	10:00 - 19:25
Paris	10:00 - 14:06
Rome	14:59 - 8:00
Zurich	10:00 - 15:00

NORWAY

Norway was the last of the Scandinavian countries to permit Jewish settlement. Despite the liberal constitution of 1814, it was not until 1851 that the ban on Jewish immigration was finally lifted. Following the pogroms in Russia in the 1880s, Jewish communities were organized in Oslo in 1892 and in Trondheim in 1905. Today, there are about 950 Jews living in Norway.

Oslo

GREAT SYNAGOGUE   13 Bjergstein   Tel. 292-612

This is Oslo's only synagogue. It was founded in 1892 and built in 1920. The second synagogue in the city was destroyed by the Nazis during the war.

The Jewish Community Center is located next door at 15 Bjergstein.

Trondheim

SYNAGOGUE & COMMUNITY CENTER

1 Arkitekt Christiesgatan

This is the most northerly synagogue in the world, only three degrees below the Arctic Circle!. It was originally built as Trondheim's main railroad station. During the war, the building was used by the Nazis as a warehouse and barracks. Its interior was desecrated, but has been restored following the war. A community center was added to the structure in 1955.

Special Note:

Sabbath candle-lighting time varies by many hours as the seasons change in this part of the world known as the "land of the midnight sun." In the winter, the Sabbath candles are lit as early as 2:00 p.m., when the sun has already set. During the long days of mid-summer, the candles are lit as late as 11:00 p.m., when the rays of the sun are still high in the sky. In some parts of Scandinavia, there are as many as 22 days of daylight during the summer months.

For further information about the Jewish community and when to light the Sabbath candles in this part of Norway, call 29-434.

KOSHER PROVISIONS

Oslo

(butcher)   *Stenberg Gate 19   Tel. 46-82-15*

RAILROAD TIMETABLE

Oslo to: Amsterdam...................11:00 - 9:54

Copenhagen.................7:40 - 17:05

Hamburg......................7:40 - 23:03

Helsinki.........................8:40 - 9:00 (next day)

Stockholm....................8:40 - 15:00

Trondheim...................8:00 - 14:38

PORTUGAL

Portugal's rulers between the 13th and 15th centuries were tolerant of the Jews. They opened their borders to the Jewish refugees from the massacres in Spain in 1391 and its Inquisition of 1492. In 1531, however, Portugal issued its own Inquisition. The Jews were given eight months to leave Portugal. Many headed for nearby North Africa while others moved to Holland and its colonies in the New World. Many Marranos (secret Jews) stayed in Portugal. Their descendents are today concentrated in the northern provinces of Tras-os-Montes, Beira Alta, and Entre-Douro-e-Minho. It is common to find Marrano families lighting Friday evening candles and then hiding them in the oven or in the basement. They have no idea that these candles were originally meant to be Sabbath candles. They claim that it has been a family tradition to light candles every Friday evening. There are about 300 Jews, not including Marranos, in Portugal today.

Belmonte

MARRANO COMMUNITY

Belmonte is located about 200 miles northeast of Lisbon. Toward the end of the 15th century all Jews in the town were forced to convert to Christianity. Those who did convert also kept their Jewish faith in the privacy of their homes. These Crypto-Jews or Marranos have survived in this town as well as in other small communities of northern and central Portugal including Argozelo, Bragança, Covilha, Lagoaça, Porto, Reboerdelo, Vilarinho and Vilarinho dos Galegos.

There are 450 Crypto-Jews in Belmonte today. Several have undergone conversion to return to Judaism.

Castelo De Vide

ANCIENT JEWISH QUARTER

The ancient Jewish quarter starts at the foot of the 13th century Castle. It consists of narrow alleyways and small houses showing the richest collection of ogival doors existing in Portugal. The restored synagogue stands in the middle of the quarter. The quarter also contains the rabbi's house, the village fountain and an oven used to bake matzohs for the holiday of Passover.

Evora

PUBLIC LIBRARY

The Public Library keeps many Hebrew manuscripts dealing with the 13th and 14th century Jewish community.

MUSEO DE EVORA

Largo do Conde de Vila Flor   Tel. 22 604

This is the most important museum in the south of Portugal. It has preserved an old Hebrew-inscribed tombstone as well as the cornerstone from the 14th century synagogue in Evora.

Faro

JEWISH CEMETERY

A 14th century cemetery is located in this southern Portugal port city.

Gouveia

MUNICIPAL MUSEUM   Rua Direita 45   Tel. 42 155

Located next to the Town Hall, the Municipal Museum has on display in its courtyard a polished granite stone with Hebrew inscriptions. It was uncovered in 1968 during the demolition of ancient houses on Rua Nova. The tablet has been identified as part of a synagogue dedicated in 1497.

Rua Nova is a street name often encountered in Portugal and recalls the "New Christians." Rua da Judiaria in Tomar also was Rua Nova.

Lisbon

ANCIENT JEWISH QUARTERS   Rua de Judiaria

This was part of the 15th cenetury Jewish quarter of the city. The ancient Jewish quarters in Lisbon were located in Alfama, the city's oldest quarter, adjacent to Largo de San Rafael and near Rua de San Miguel. The largest Jewish quarter was located in the area where today's Rua da Madalena lies; another quarter was in the old San Sebastio de Pedreira section; and the fourth Jewish quarter, known as the Petite Juiverie, was in the block of houses which now extends between the Church of San Juliao and the Bank of Portugal building.

SYNAGOGA SHAARE TIKVA

59 Rua Alexandre Herculano   Tel. 681-592

The Sephardic synagogue of Lisbon was built in 1902 and was designed in the Moorish-Reivival style.

JEWISH COMMUNITY CENTER

10 Rua Rosa Araujo   Tel. 57 20 41

Opened in 1948, the Jewish Community Center serves to link the older Sephardic Jews and the newer Ashkenazic Jews who came to Portugal as refugees in the late 1930s and early 1940s.

Porto

KADOORIE SYNAGOGA   340 Rua Guerra Junqueiro

Kahal Kodesh Mekor Haim Synagogue was built by the Kadoorie family (of Bagdad) in the 1920s.

Tomar

MEDIEVAL SYNAGOGUE   Rua Nova

Located in the old Jewish quarter, this former synagogue was used as a wine cellar for centuries. It is now a national landmark and a museum. The prayer hall measures 9.5 x 8.2 meters with groin vaulting which rest on four thin cylindrical piers forming a square bay in the center of the room.

There are mouldings from ancient tombstones (14th century) as well as the cornerstone of a 13th century synagogue known as the Belmonte Synagogue.

NATIONAL MUSEUM OF ANCIENT ART

Rua das Janelas Verdes   Tel. 67 27 25

There are several paintings depicting scenes relating to Jewish ritual.

KOSHER PROVISIONS

Lisbon   Rabbi Abraham Assor

Rua Rodrigo da Fonseca 38-1   DTO   Tel. 53-03-96

Porto

Rua Rodrigues   Lobo 98   Tel.65535

(butcher) *Rua da Escola Politechnica 279   Tel. 652450*

SYNAGOGUES

Lisbon

(Sephardic)   *59 Rua Alexandre Herculano   Tel. 6815-92*

(Ashkenazic)   *110 Rua Elias Garcia   Tel. 7752-83*

RAILROAD TIMETABLE

Lisbon to:		
Barcelona	8:10 - 8:08	
Bordeaux	15:10 - 14:10	
Faro	9:10 - 12:55	
Geneva	16:00 - 9:28	
Madrid	7:30 - 18:40	
Paris	15:10 - 19:15	(next day)
Porto	11:00 - 14:00	
Seville	8:25 - 20:53	

SPAIN

It is said that the Jews first came to Spain, *Sfarad*, after the destruction of the Holy Temple in Jerusalem in 586 B.C.E. The Visigoths, who occupied Spain in the 5th century, embraced Christianity, and persecuted its Jewish and Moslem population. The Moslems (Moors and Berbers), from North Africa, conquered Spain in 711. It was during this Moslem rule that the Jews prospered to such a great degree that the era became known as the "Golden Age of Spain." Under the caliphs, the Jews produced poets, philosophers, scientists, scholars, statesmen, financiers, and royal advisers. The Jewish scholars translated into Hebrew and Latin the classical Greek writings which were written in Arabic. These classical writings would reappear in a new era, the Renaissance. Some eminent Jews in medieval Spain include Moses Maimonides (Rambam), Yehudah Halevi, Benjamin of Tudela, and Isaac Abrabanel.

The Christian rulers drove most of the Moslems from Spain by the beginning of the 13th century. This was known as the *Reconquista*. In 1391, the Christian mobs annihilated the Jewish quarters of Seville, Barcelona, Cordoba, and Toledo. This was the beginning of the end of Jewish settlement in Spain. Jews at this time chose to publicly convert to Christianity and would actually eat pork in the public squares to prove their outward Christianity. However, in the privacy of their homes, they would still practice their Jewish faith. In later years, the Inquisitors (secret police) would patrol through the streets with pieces of pork. As they approached a suspected *converso,* they would push a piece of pork in his face. If the suspect would eat it immediately, he was spared. If, however, when the Inquisitors would hold the pork and say, "Marrano, Marrano," (which means pork in Spanish) and the suspect would turn his head away, he was immediately taken into custody. The term "Marrano" has since come to signify these secret Jews, who would convert to Christianity in public but become secret Jews in private.

The Inquisition was established in 1478. It sought to destroy these Marranos with every type of weapon, including death by torture. On March 30, 1492, King Ferdinand V and Queen Isabella signed the decree expelling all Jews from Spain. The Jews were given four months, until August 1, 1492 to leave. This was the day of *Tish'a Ba'av,* the fast of the ninth day of the Hebrew month of Av, which commemorates the destruction of the first and second Holy Temples in Jerusalem.

The Inquisition was not officially abolished until 1868. The Inquisition was instituted in all colonies of Spain, including southern Italy, Sicily, and Sardinia, the New World colonies of New Spain (Mexico and southwest United States) and South America.

Sephardic Jews from North Africa and Greece were the first Jews to resettle in Spain. During the 1930s and 1940s, Francisco Franco, admitted as many as 40,000 Jews from Nazi-occupied territories in Europe. It has been rumored that Franco was descended from Marranos. There are about 12,000 Jews living in Spain today. The largest communities are in Madrid and Barcelona.

Avila

CHURCH OF TODOS LOS SANTOS

Calle Bracamonte

This building was originally built as a synagogue. The Chapel of Mosen Rubi, located at Calle de Lopez Numez, was also a former synagogue.

Barcelona

CASA SEFARDITA   24 Calle Porvenir   Tel. 200-61-48

Spain's second largest city, Barcelona, has a Jewish

population of over 5,000. The first synagogue building on Spanish soil since the expulsion of 1492, was erected in 1954. The synagogue houses a Sephardic congregation on the first floor and an Ashkenazic congregation on the third floor. There is also a Jewish Community Center which contains facilities for cultural and recreational activities.

CARRER DELL CALL

A street located in the oldest section of the city was once the Juderia, the Jewish quarter. In Catalan, the word "Call" means *kahal,* or congregation or synagogue.

MONTJUICH

Barcelona is cradled between two hills, Tibidabo and Montjuich. Montjuich is the Catalan word for "Mountain of the Jews." In the 11th and 12th centuries, many Jews owned land on the slopes of this mountain. Here too was a Jewish cemetery which was abandoned after the massacres of 1391. Some tombstones from this cemetery are on display in a special room in the Historical Museum of Barcelona, which is located in the city's Old Gothic quarter. It was on this same Montjuich that the 1992 Olympics were held.

Béjar

ANCIENT SYNAGOGUES

Calle de 29 de Agosto (Numbers 3, 5, 7)

This was the location of ancient synagogues. They were located near the Palace of the Dukes.

Besalu

ANCIENT MIKVEH

A 14th century mikveh (ritual bath) is located near the bridgehead (which is approached by a passage and 36 steps).

Burgos

Burgos was the largest Jewish community in Old Castile in the 11th century. It was an important center of trade. It was here that the Cid imposed on Jewish moneylenders by leaving an iron-bound chest filled with sand rather than gold as a surety for a loan to finance his campaigns. He later did honestly redeem his pledge. The actual "Cofre del Cid," according to tradition, may be seen in the Cloister of the Cathedral.

After the pogrom of 1391, a number of Jews were ostensibly converted and settled in a special Converso quarter called the *Barriada de San Esteban*. During the next century the majority of those who remained gradually became amalgamated with the Christians. Among them was the Converso bishop, *Pablo de Santa Maria* (ca. 1350-1435), known prior to his baptism in 1390 as Salomon Halevi. He became bishop of Burgos in 1415, having previously been its chief rabbi!

Caceres

ANCIENT SYNAGOGUE

The Espiritu Santo, Ermita de San Antonio is a church which was built on the site of a 13th century synagogue.

Calahorra

MEDIEVAL SYNAGOGUE   Calle de la Sinagogue

The Church of San Francisco was originally built as a synagogue.

Carmona

CHURCH OF SAN BLAS   Calle de la Juderia

This church at one time was a synagogue.

Ciudad Real

CHURCH OF SAN JUAN BAUTISTA

This church was originally built as a synagogue.

Cordoba

ALMODOVER GATE

This was the entrance into the old Jewish quarter. It was known as the *Bah-ah-Yahud* or "Gate of the Jews."

CALLE JUDA LEVI

This street was named in honor of Yehudah ha-Levi, the medieval poet who was born in Toledo in 1075 but lived most of his life in Cordoba.

MAIMONIDES (RAMBAM) STATUE

Moshe ben Maimon was born in Cordoba in 1135. At the age of thirteen, Maimonides and his family fled the city when the Almohades, fanatical Berber tribesmen from North Africa, crossed the Straits of Gibraltar and conquered Cordoba.

Maimonides became the noted theologian, philosopher, and physician. His monumental works, the *Mishneh Torah* and the *Guide to the Perplexed,* were written in North Africa. His sojourns include Fez, Morocco, Alexandria, Egypt, and finally, to his resting place in Tiberias, Israel. The Maimonides statue was erected by the Spanish government in 1964. In 1985, many nations issued special commemorative stamps in honor of the 850th anniversary of the birth of Maimonides.

RAMBAM SYNAGOGUE   20 Calle de los Judios

A small Moorish building built in 1315 is now a national monument. From the women's gallery, one can see the handsomely carved plasterwork above the niche where the Holy Ark stood and where the Torah scrolls were kept. A Hebrew inscription on the wall establishes the name of the founder or donor, Isaac Moheb. After the expulsion of the Jews in 1492, the synagogue was converted into a quarantine hospital for victims of rabies, an oratory for the guild of shoemakers and, centuries later, was converted into the Church of St. Crispin. The building was partially restored in 1935 as a synagogue in commemoration of the 800th anniversary of the birth of Maimonides.

Elche

The remains of a 6th century synagogue, complete with a mosaic floor, are located near Puerta de Santo Polo.

Estella

CURCH OF SANTA MARIA JUS DEL CASTILLO

This church was built in 1262 as a Jewish house of worship.

Gerona

ANCIENT JEWISH QUARTER   Calle San Lorenzo

This city was the center of Kabbalism in Spain. Nachmanides (Ramban) lived in Gerona during the 13th century. The Jewish cemetery was on the hillside known as Montjuich.

Granada

The 10th century Arab historians called this city *Gharnatat al-Yahud*, "Granada of the Jews." It has been said, "Whoever has not seen the splendor of the Jews of Granada, their fortune and their glory, has never seen true glory." This description applies most aptly to Shmuel ha-Nagid (993-1055), who was a field commander of the army, Talmud scholar, Hebrew poet, mathematician, and philosopher. His son, Joseph ibn-Naghdela, built the oldest sections of the Alhambra, Spain's most beautiful palace and fortress.

ALHAMBRA

Built on a hill, this palace-fortress is a city in itself. Massive walls and towers served to protect the exquisite chambers and luxurious courtyards within. The beauty of the interior almost defies description. From the marble floors, graceful columns draw the eye upward to the ceilings.

Through the artistry of the builders, such commonplace

*The Edict of Expulsion was signed in the Alhambra
on March 30, 1492.*

materials as stucco, plaster, and wood are converted into lacy patterns of great delicacy. It was within the walls of this luxurious palace that the fate of the Jews of Spain was decreed. On March 30, 1492, the Edict of Expulsion was signed in the Hall of the Ambassadors. This harsh decree, urged upon Ferdinand and Isabella by Tomas de Torquemada, the Grand Inquisitor, required that the Jews convert to Catholicism or leave the country within four months.

As many as 160,000 Jews chose to leave, uprooting themselves from their homes and livelihoods, and leaving behind all they had built up over the centuries, rather than renounce their faith. It was also in this Hall of the Ambassadors in 1492 that Ferdinand and Isabella put their names to the agreement that sponsored the voyage of Christopher Columbus across the Atlantic to the New World. It is believed that there were several Marranos (secret Jews) aboard Columbus' vessel.

Guadalajara

ANCIENT JEWISH CEMETERY

This city was the birthplace of Moses de Leon (1240-1305), author of *Sefer ha-Zohar*. The cemetery was located in the vicinity of the Calle de Madrid and the Hospital Provincial. The synagogue was located on Calle de la Sinagogue, adjacent to the Church of San Pedro Y San Pablo.

Hervas

ANCIENT JEWISH QUARTER

There is a Calle Rabilero, rabbi's street; Calle de la Sinagogue (#1 was the site of the synagogue); and Casa de los Diezmos (house of the tithes), where the Jews paid their taxes.

Lucena

CHURCH OF SANTIAGO

This church was said to have been built as a synagogue.

Madrid

JEWISH COMMUNITY CENTER

3 Calle Balmes   Tel. 445-95-35

After 1868, Jews were permitted to settle freely in Madrid, but it was not until the 1920s that the Jewish community was in any way organized. Madrid was the asylum for some Jewish refugees during World War I and again in the 1930s. On December 17, 1968, four hundred and seventy-six years after the Jews were expelled, the first house of worship was built in Spain's capital. The synagogue, located near the Plaza de Sorollla, houses a school, community center, meeting hall, mikveh, and a kosher restaurant. Please note that it is necessary to make reservations for meals.

JUDERIA

The old Jewish quarters of Madrid were located along Calle de la Fe, Calle de Bailen, Plaza de Oriente, and Plaza de Lavapics.

Majorca

MONTESION CHURCH

This church was built on the foundations of the Great Synagogue of Palma and has been used for centuries almost exclusively by the *Chuetas*. The *Chuetas* are descendents of Jews who were forcibly converted in 1435. Although they have been practicing Catholics for more than five hundred years, they have remained, for the most part, a separate sect. They live in Palma and many own jewelry shops on the Calle de las Platerias (street of silver shops). The word "Chueta" is derived from *Chuya*, "pork eater," since the *Chuetas* ate pork publicly to demonstrate their adherence to Christianity. The local merchants call the *Chuetas*, "Judios" or "Hebreos."

PALMA CATHEDRAL

Among the treasures of this cathedral, which was built in 1239, are a handsome pair of 14th century *rimonim* or silver Torah finials. For many years these were carried aloft on poles in church processions. Even more impressive is the giant candelabrum suspended from the vaulted ceiling of the cathedral. This elegant candelabrum came from the Great Synagogue of Palma. It contains 350 lights and is a poignant reminder of the grandeur of the ancient Jewish house of worship.

Malaga

The *Costa del Sol*, Spain's famous "sun coast," extends from Algeciras, in the west to Almeria, 72 miles of picturesque shoreline hugging the Mediterranean.

SOLOMON IBN GABIROL STATUE

In a park in the center of Malaga (near the harbor) stands the statue of Solomon ibn Gabirol (1021-1069), the foremost Hebrew poet of Spain. The statue was erected by the municipality in 1969, to mark the 900th anniversary of the great poet's death. It was designed by the American sculptor, Reed Armstrong.

By the age of sixteen, ibn Gabirol already showed signs of genius in his secular poetry about the joys of love and wine. However, he is best remembered for his religious poems, many of which have been incorporated into the liturgy of the prayerbook. Although his reputation rested solely on his poetry, Solomon ibn Gabirol was also a great philosopher. His major philosophical work was the *Fountain of Life*.

SYNAGOGUE   4 Duquesa de Parcent   Tel. 21-40-41

There are approximately 1,000 Jews in Malaga today. The synagogue is located at 4 Duquesa de Parcent. There are daily religious services. The building also houses a Hebrew school.

Marbella

CONGREGATION BETH EL

Calle Palmera 20   Tel. 77-15-86

Many Jews are involved in the tourist industry along the *Costa del Sol*. There is a modest facility for worship in Torremolinos and a beautiful new synagogue building in the tract of villas called Urbanizacion El Real on the outskirts of Marbella. This small synagogue has an interesting history.

The large Ohayon family built the synagogue to serve their own religious needs and those of other Jews in the area. Congregation Beth El is the first synagogue in Spain with a Hebrew inscription on its front façade. Its universal message, taken from the Psalms, reads, "My house shall be called a house of prayer for all people."

Medinaceli

CHURCH OF SAN ROMAN
This church was originally built as a synagogue.

Miranda de Ebro

MEDIEVAL SYNAGOGUE   18 Calle de la Puenta
The old Juderia was near the Calle de la Independencia.

Ona

ANCIENT JEWISH QUARTER   Calle Barriso
The Juderia was located on Calle Barriso, to the left of the Arch de la Estrella, towards Plaza Mayor. The second house on the right-hand side, with an overhanging story, was originally a synagogue.

Paredes de Nava

IGLESIA CRISTO DE LA BELLA CRUX
This church was originally designed as a synagogue.

Segovia

CHURCH OF CORPUS CHRISTI

Originally the main synagogue of Segovia, it was converted into the Church of Corpus Christi in 1420 because the Jews allegedly desecrated the Host. The structure was built in the 13th century, designed in the Mudejar style, and resembles the Santa Maria la Blanca in Toledo. In 1572, the building became the property of Franciscan nuns and was very seriously damaged by a fire in 1899. It has since been restored.

ANCIENT JEWISH QUARTERS

The Calle de la Juderia and the Calle de la Juderia Nueva (Barrio Nuevo) are the sites of the old and new ancient Jewish quarters. The old quarter was located between the cathedral and the city walls.

CHURCH DE LA MERCED

This church was originally built as a synagogue.

EL FONSARIO

An ancient Jewish cemetery is said to have been in the Valley of the Clamores, below the city wall, once buttressing the Juderia.

Seville

EL BARRIO DE SANTA CRUZ

Not far from the cathedral is the *Arco de Juderia* which was the gateway to the Jewish quarter of Seville. During the 14th century, there were twenty-three synagogues in the city serving over 7,000 Jewish families. In 1391, a series of violent anti-Jewish attacks took place, fomented by Ferrant Marinez, a high church official. The massacres and mass conversions obliterated Jewish life in the city.

Several streets still recall the names of this once-vibrant Jewish community: *Calle de Cal*, Street of the Kahal or Congregation; *Calle de Cal Major*, Street of the Large Congregation; *Juderia Vieja,* the old Jewish quarter; and *Calle de los Tintes*, Street of the Dyers. The trade of tinting and dyeing was almost exclusively carried on by Jews.

Several other churches in Seville were probably former synagogues. They include the Church of Santa Maria Blanca, the Convent of Madre de Dios, and the Church of Santa Cruz.

ANCIENT JEWISH CEMETERY

The ancient Jewish cemetery is located in the Macerena district. There are several 13th and 14th century Jewish tombstones within these present-day Christian burial grounds.

CHRISTOPHER COLUMBUS ARCHIVES

(Archives of Indies)   3 Avenida Queipo de Llano

Many of Columbus' backers were Marranos or secret Jews. Several of his crew-men on his voyage to the New World were reported to also have been Marranos. Columbus sailed his ships up the Guadalquivir River and docked at the inland port of Seville upon his triumphant return from the New World. Columbus is buried in the cathedral across the street from the Archives of Indies.

Siguenza

MEDIEVAL SYNAGOGUES

There were medieval synagogues located at 6 Calle de la Sinagoga and at 12 Calle de San Vicente.

Toledo   ·

Toledo has been compared to Jerusalem. The walled city is perched on a rocky cliff and its buildings are designed with golden-hued limestone. At its height, the Jewish community of Toledo was one of the largest and most influential in Spain. In the 12th century there were more than 12,000 Jews, nine synagogue, and five midrashim (small chapels). Toledo was an important center of Jewish learning and literature. It was the home of the famous "School of Translators" which included Jewish, Christian, and Moslem scholars. Among the many outstanding Jewish scholars and writers in Toledo were:

* Abraham ibn Ezra (1092-1167), an important grammarian and interpreter of the Bible. To this day, his commentaries accompany the text in most of the scholarly editions of the Hebrew Bible.

* Yehudah ha-Levi (ca.1086-1145), physician, philosopher, and poet. Many of his religious poems have become part of the prayerbook used in the synagogue on the High Holy Days. In his stirring poem, *Ode to Zion*, Yehudah ha-Levi voices his yearning for the Jews to return to the land of their fathers,

Israel. He is also known for his philosophical treatise, the *Kusari*.

* Rabbi Asher bar Rav Yechiel (Rosh) was born in Germany in 1250. He offered to be jailed instead of his rabbi and teacher, Rabbi Meir of Rothenburg (see Worms, Germany). The Rosh moved to Toledo in 1305 where he served as rabbi until his death in 1328.

* Rabbi Jacob bar Rav Asher (Tur) came to Spain from Germany in 1305 with his father, the Rosh. His scholarly work was concerned with combining all laws discussed in the Babylonian and Jerusalem Talmuds.

SANTA MARIA LA BLANCA

Calle de los Reyes Catolicos

The oldest Jewish monument in Toledo stands in a quiet garden in what was once the heart of the Juderia. It was built in the 13th century and was originally the Great Synagogue of Toledo. The exterior is not impressive, however, the interior is very somber and awe-inspiring.

The space mearures 92 feet by 75 feet and is 41 feet in height. There are four aisles with 32 graceful octagonal pillars supporting a long vista of horseshoe-shaped arches. The elaborate capitals are molded in plaster and ornamented with pine-cone motifs. During the 13th century, Spain was covered with extensive pine forests. On the bases of some of the columns and on the pavement are ancient tiles. The doors and ceiling are of larchwood. There is no women's section or gallery.

Santa Maria la Blanca Synagogue.

The synagogue has undergone many changes over the centuries. It was used as a refuge for reformed prostitutes, as a barracks and storeroom in the 1790s, as a dance hall, a carpenter's workshop, and as a church - Santa Maria la Blanca. Even after so many centuries and desecrations, there is still one solitary Star of David which has somehow survived to this day. It is located, as a plaster frieze, above the horseshoe arch, in the northwest quadrant of the building. The Santa Maria la Blanca is now a national museum.

The remains of an ancient mikveh is located about 30 meters east of the Santa Maria la Blanca.

EL TRANSITO SYNAGOGUE   Calle Samuel Levi

Samuel Levi Abulafia, for whom the street was named, was treasurer and close advisor to King Pedro I. In 1357, Don Pedro granted Abulafia permission to build this private chapel for his family. The El Transito Synagogue is a single-nave hall measuring 76 feet by 31 feet and is 39 feet in height.

Adjoining the synagogue on the eastern side was Abulafia's private residence, which is no longer standing. Another building close by, at one time the residence of El Greco and now the El Greco Museum, was also part of Abulafia's property.

An underground passage is said to exist along the outer edge of the Juderia, which was supposed to be used as an escape route by both Jews and Marranos. Samuel Levi Abulafia's palace (site of today's El Greco Museum) had a tunnel leading to the banks of the Tagus River. Unfortunately, he did not have a chance to use it as an escape route. In 1361, King

Pedro I turned against Abulafia and accused him of cheating the royal exchequer. Abulafia was imprisoned in Seville and was tortured to death.

The El Transito Synagogue is considered to be the best preserved monument of the pre-Inquisition period. The ceiling, made of cedar-of-Lebanon, is ornamented with Hebrew calligraphy. The filigreed plaster decorations on the walls and cornices contain Hebrew inscriptions and quotations from the Bible and from the Psalms.

The eastern wall, encrusted with arabesque panels, is dominated by a rectangular windowed niche, in front of which stand three foliated arches on slim colonettes. On the southern wall are galleries which contained the women's section. The gallery along the western wall is said to have been the choir loft. Above the galleries runs the broad ornamental frieze. Above the frieze, a windowed arcade runs along the four walls of the hall.

The side wall arcades contain alternating windows and blind arches. The arrangement along the eastern wall, however, is completely different; here two windows are set side by side in the center, which in both shape and position suggest the twin tablets of the law. The panels on either side of the Ark niche display elaborate inscriptions in Hebrew containing praise of King Pedro and Abulafia.

In 1492, the building was given to a military order, the Knights of Calatrava. There are Christian tombs of members of this order within the El Transito Synagogue. The Inquisition transformed the synagogue into the Church of

Notre Dame, hence the name "Transito," transition. In 1550, the building became an asylum. In 1798, it was converted into barracks. In 1877, the synagogue building was declared a national monument.

Adjoining the synagogue is the Museum of Sephardic Culture which was established by the Spanish government in 1971.

EL GRECO MUSEUM (Casa de El Greco)

A short distance from the El Transito Synagogue stands the so-called Casa de El Greco. This was the site of Samuel Levi Abulafia's palace. The palace was replaced by several other buildings on the same site. The Casa de El Greco was built at the turn of the 20th century by Marques de Vega-Inclan and resembles a 16th century Manchego mansion.

JEWISH CEMETERY

The ancient Jewish cemetery is located on the road to the present-day Christian cemetery, behind the Instituto de Ensenanza Media, at the Cerro de la Horca.

CALLE DE SYNAGOGUE

The small street located off the Calle Hombre de Palo (north of the cathedral), was the site of one of Toledo's nine synagogues.

Valencia

CHURCH OF SAN CRISTOBAL   Calle del Mar

This church was originally built as a synagogue.

Vic

ANCIENT JEWISH QUARTER

The Juderia and the synagogue were located between the cathedral and the Castillo de Moncada (Plaza d'en Guiu).

Zamora

MEDIEVAL SYNAGOGUE   15 Calle Ignacio Gazapo

There was a medieval synagogue at this location, which is east of the Church of Santa Lucia.

Zaragoza

CHURCH OF SAN CARLOS

Calle de Don Jaime I & Calle de Coso

This building was originally built as a synagogue.

KOSHER PROVISIONS

Madrid

Calle Balmes 3   Tel. 445-95-35

Lubavitch   *22 Abascal   Tel. 441-5430*

Malaga

(butcher)   *Armengual de la Motta 20   Tel. 27-10-82*

Kosher Costa   *Arango 5   Tel. 27-62 49*

Torremolinos

(butcher)   *Loma de Los Riscos 11   Tel. 38-79-51*

SYNAGOGUES

Alicante   *Calle Ramon y Cajal 9/7   (Mr. Cohen)*

Barcelona   *Calle Porvenir 24   Tel. 200-61-48*

Ceuta (North Africa)

Calle Sargento Coriat 8   Tel. 51-32-13

Madrid

Calle Balmes 3   Tel. 445-95-35

Chabad House (Lubavitch)

Calle Jordan 9 (Apt. 4)   Tel. 445-96-29

Malaga   *Calle Duquesa de Parcent 4   Tel. 21-40-41*

Marbella   *Calle Palmera 20   Tel. 77-15-86*

Melilla (North Africa)

Calle General Mola 19   Tel. 68-16-00

Palma de Mallorca

Apartado de Correos 39   Tel. 23-86-86

Santa Cruz de Tenerife

Calle Villalba Hervas 3   Tel. 24-77-81

Seville   *Calle Peral 10   Tel. 25-81-00 ext. 324*

Torremolinos (Malaga)

Calle Skal (La Roca)   Tel. 38-39-52

Valencia

Calle Ausias March 42, Puerta 35   Tel. 334-34-16

MIKVEHS

Barcelona   *Calle Porvenir 24   Tel. 200-61-48*
Madrid   *Calle Balmes 3   Tel. 445-95-35*
Marbella   *Calle Palmera 20   Tel. 77-15-86*

RAILROAD TIMETABLE

Madrid to: Barcelona............ 11:10 - 20:00

Geneva................ 8:00 - 8:53 (next day)

Lisbon................. 10:15 - 19:05

Marseille............. 22:40 - 16:39

Nice...................... 22:40 - 20:09

Paris.................... 8:00 - 23:21

Rome................... 8:00 - 20:05 (next day)

SWEDEN

In 1774, the enlightened King Gustav III, revoked anti-Jewish ordinances of his predecessors and invited Jewish settlement. Jews settled in Stockholm, Gothenburg, Malmo, Norrkoping, Lund, and Uppsala. It was not until 1870 that Sweden's Jews achieved complete political emancipation and basic acceptance as citizens and members of the community.

During World War II, the Swedish government helped in the rescue of thousands of Jewish refugees, especially of the near 8,000 Danish Jews. Sweden has the largest Jewish population in Scandinavia, about 16,000. In 1988, the Swedish government placed a ban on *shchitah* or ritual slaughter of all animals.

Gothenburg

GREAT SYNAGOGUE

Ostra Larmgatan 12   Tel. 13-67-78

The oldest existing synagogue building in Sweden was constructed in 1855. The community itself dates from 1780. Adjoining this Liberal synagogue is the Jewish Community Center, which houses a kosher restaurant, religious school, and a small chapel used by Orthodox worshippers for daily prayers.

Malmo

SYNAGOGUE   Foreningsgatan & Betianaplan

It was in this seventy-five-year-old synagogue that the last Jewish refugees from Denmark arrived, on Yom Kippur eve, in 1943, in time to join the congregation in the traditional *Kol Nidre* service.

JEWISH COMMUNITY CENTER

Kamrergatan 11   Tel. 11-84-60

This community center houses a home for the aged, mikveh, library, and youth facilities.

Stockholm

SITE OF FIRST SYNAGOGUE   19 Sjalagardsgatan

The present-day museum for Lapp culture was originally built as Stokholm's first synagogue. The women's gallery is still intact.

GREAT SYNAGOGUE

Wahrendorffsgatan 3   Tel. 23-51-60

The Great Synagogue is the largest in the country. It was built in 1870 and designed by the Swedish architect Frederik Vilhelm Scholander. It is an oblong structure with galleries and a flat skylighted ceiling, instead of vaults. The large, tall windows in the aisles and in the galleries admit ample daylight. Triangular window-heads take the place of pointed arches. Still of medieval inspiration are the rose window and the bracketed cornice; but the overall impression is one of efficiency and concern for space and light. The decoration of the gallery parapet anticipates the freer design of the English Arts and Crafts movement of the 1880s.

The congregation follows an Orthodox/Conservative ritual. The men and women are seated separately but the organ is used during services and a Conservative-style prayerbook is used.

JEWISH CEMETERIES

The oldest Jewish cemeteries, dating from the late 18th century, are located in the Kungsholm section of the city, at Igelddammsgatan, Alstromergatan, and Kronobergsgatan. The newest Jewish cemetery is located at Hagaparken, in the suburb of Solna.

JUDAICA HOUSE   Nybrogatan 19   Tel. 63-65-66

The Judaica House incorporates a Jewish Community Center, Hebrew school, library, kosher dairy cafeteria, gymnasium, and meeting rooms.

KOSHER PROVISIONS

Gothenburg

Larmgatan 12   Tel. 13-67-78

(butcher) *Stampgatan 68   Tel. 15-55-49*

Malmo

(grocery) *Carl Herslowsgatan 7   Tel. 23-55-15*

(butcher) *Skolgatan 2   Tel. 97-68-00*

Stockholm

Nybrogatan 19   Tel. 63-65-66

(grocery) *Tjarhusgatan 5*   *Tel. 42-80-30*

(restaurant) *Vastgotagatan 16*   *Tel. 44-87-50*

SYNAGOGUES

Gothenburg

Andra Langgatan 16

 Liberal Congregation   *Ostra Larmgatan 12   Tel. 13-67-78*

Helsingborg   Springposttgranden 4

Lund   *Winstrupsgatan 1   Tel. 14-80-52*

Malmo   *Foreningsgatan & Betianaplan*

Stockholm

Great Synagogue   *Wahrendorffsgatan 3   Tel. 23-51-60*

Adas Jeshurun   *Nybrogatan 12   Tel. 61-82-82*

Adas Yisroel   *St. Paulsgatan 13   Tel. 44-19-95*

MIKVEH

Malmo   *Kamrergatan 11*   *Tel. 11-84-60*

RAILROAD TIMETABLE

Stockholm to: Amsterdam.............11:13 - 9:54

Copenhagen...........7:13 - 15:21

Frankfurt................15:13 - 12:31

Oslo.........................7:00 - 13:25

Paris........................7:13 - 8:38 (next day)

Trondheim..............7:45 - 22:05

Vienna.....................15:13 - 21:28

SWITZERLAND

The first mention of Jews living in Switzerland was in Basel, in the year 1213, when it was one of the major Jewish communities in the Holy Roman Empire. Jews migrated to Switzerland from Alsace and southern Germany on the one hand, and from France on the other. The stream of immigration gained in intensity after the expulsion of Jews from France in 1306. The principal occupation of these groups of Jews was moneylending. The life of the Jews until 1348 was relatively free of any major upheavals, with the exception of Bern, where, as a result of a blood libel (ca. 1294), some Jews were executed and the rest expelled. The Ogre Fountain in Bern still stands as a bitter reminder of the blood libel - that Jewish "monsters" sacrificed Christian children on Good Friday.

In 1348, the whole of Swiss Jewry was threatened with extermination. The Black Plague having reached the countryside around Lake Geneva (Savoy), a number of Jews in the town of Chillon were tortured to confess to having caused the plague by poisoning the wells. As each town throughout Switzerland, and in all of Europe, was struck by the plague, the Jews were burnt at the stake.

In 1622, all Jews were banished from Switzerland. Only Jewish physicians were permitted to remain. After 1648, some Jews started moving into the northern canton of Aargau, and lived in the two villages of Lengnau and Endingen. They were not permitted to own land but were permitted to trade, buy, and sell at fairs and markets. Many of the Jews of these two villages were cattle dealers. They were the Jewish cowboys of Switzerland.

Influenced by the ideas of the French Revolution, the proclamation of the Helvetian Republic (1798) was a turning point in the history of Swiss Jewry. Jews were now granted partial freedom of movement, residence, and trade, with full freedom of religion granted in 1874.

During the 1930s, Switzerland gave refuge to 40,000 Jews from Germany. They were, however, placed in internment camps for the duration of the war. The Nazis did not invade Switzerland since the Swiss threatened to blow up the vital alpine passes, through which the Germans were shipping military armaments to its southern ally, Italy. There are today about 20,000 Jews living in Switzerland.

Switzerland does not permit the ritual slaughter of animals. Jews must therefore import all of their kosher meats from France and Holland.

Basel

STADT-CASINO   14 Steinenberg

This is the building in which Theodor Herzl convened the first World Zionist Congress, in August, 1897. This was the launching of the political movement which led to the establishment of the State of Israel in 1948. There is a bronze plaque on the wall to the right of the stage. This concert hall is still in operation and is not open to the public except during concerts.

KONIGE HOTEL (THREE KINGS HOTEL)

Located in the old city of Basel, the Drei Konig Hotel was founded in 1026 and is said to be the oldest hotel in Switzerland. This national monument has been visited by Napoleon, Voltaire, Metternich, and Theodor Herzl.

ANCIENT SYNAGOGUE SITES   9 & 21 Unterer Heuberg

These two addresses are believed to have been former synagogue locations. The courtyard of 33 Heuberg contains former Jewish tombstones.

BASEL JEWISH MUSEUM

Kornhausgasse 8   Tel. 25-95-14

This is the only Jewish museum in Switzerland. It contains artifacts from the former Jewish communities of Lengnau and Endingen, ancient Hebrew books, and many photographs from the First Zionist Congress. There are also several fragments from ancient Jewish tombstones from 1222.

The museum is open Mondays and Wednesdays from 3:00 to 5:00 p.m. and on Sundays from 10:00 a.m. to 12 noon and from 3:00 to 5:00 p.m.

GREAT SYNAGOGUE
24 Leimenstrasse   Tel. 228-700

The Basel Great Synagogue was built in 1868. It was designed by Hermann Gauss in the Moorish Revival style. The original building had only one central dome. In 1891, the structure was enlarged. There are now two large bulbous domes. The interior is lavish. The rabbi's pulpit is raised on a wooden pedestal. The stained-glass window above the Ark portrays a snow crystal in bright reds, yellows, and blues.

The Jewish Community Center, Hebrew School, library, and kosher restaurant are located in the adjoining building. There is an additional synagogue located at Ahornstrasse 14.

Bern

OGRE FOUNTAIN (DIE KINDERFRESSBRUNNER)

The Fountain of the Ogre is a bitter reminder of life during the Middle Ages in Switzerland. The Jews were required to wear special clothing. The Jews' hat or *Judenhut* was one such garment. The term *Yekkeh*, is derived from the special jacket or coat which was required to be worn by Jews in certain German towns. In 1294, the Christians of Bern accused the Jews of kidnapping their children, killing them, and using their blood to bake *matzot* for Passover. This blood libel was repeated many times during the Middle Ages, resulting in entire Jewish communities throughout Europe being uprooted and driven out.

The Ogre Fountain depicts, very graphically, the Jewish "monster" sacrificing Christian children on Good Friday.

Endingen - Lengnau

These two villages were first established after 1648, when Jews were permitted to live only in this part of Switzerland. The Jews were mostly involved with cattle trading. The oldest synagogue in Switzerland, located in the town square of Lengnau, was built in 1847. It was recently restored and is now used only on special anniversary celebrations. Some of the original Jewish homes are located just to the left of the synagogue. There are no Jews today in this town. Yet, the former Jewish homes still bear the marks of where the *mezuzahs* were placed on the doorposts. There is a Jewish Rest Home in Lengnau. The key to the synagogue is located with the Rest Home administrator, Tel. (056) 51 12 03.

About one half mile from Lengnau, in the direction of Endingen, is the old Jewish cemetery. It is recognized by a cluster of trees, on the right side of the road, and is surrounded by a stone wall. During the first years of settlement in Lengnau, the Jews were forbidden to bury their dead in Switzerland. They had to travel north, to the Rhine River, and bury their dead on an island in the middle of the river, known as *Juden Insle*, Jews' Island.

Endingen was truly a Jewish *shtetl* or village. There still are no churches in the town. The tallest structure in town is the synagogue which was built in 1850. It is the only synagogue designed with bells built into its façade. These bells would toll in times of impending danger. The bells still chime, but only to signal the time of day. In order to visit the synagogue contact Mr. J. Bloch at Buckstrasse 2, Tel. (056) 52 15 46

These two towns are located near Baden. There are buses that leave from the central railroad station in Baden.

Geneva

GREAT SYNAGOGUE   Place de la Synagogue

This synagogue is located in the center of the city. There is a plaque in front of the synagogue which is dedicated to the victims of the Holocaust.

SEPHARDIC SYNAGOGUE

54 route de Malagnou   Tel. (022) 736-96-32

Congregation Hekhal Haness was built into a hillside. There is lush vegetation landscaped on the terraced retaining walls. The large white box sitting on top of the synagogue is actually a skylight designed with a thin veneer of white marble. This is the only source of natural light in the main sanctuary. The building was built with the asistance of Mr. Gaon who owns the luxurious Noga Hotel on Lake Geneva. (If you change the letters of Gaon, you get Noga).

The lavish interior of the synagogue contains mahogany wall panels, crystal chandeliers, and plush theatre seating. There is a small daily chapel, exquisite banquet hall, gym, and three mikvehs.

There are daily services in this Orthodox congregation. There is also a *shteeble* (Machsikei Hadass) in Geneva located at 2, Place des Eaux Vives (Tel. 47 14 38). The Jewish Community Center of Geneva is located at 10, rue St. Leger (Tel. 20 46 86).

St. Moritz

For those who enjoy the Swiss Alps, St. Moritz is just one of several resorts which caters to Jewish travelers. The winter crowd is geared to the skiers. It is extremely cold in the winter due to the strong prevailing winds. Many prefer Arosa, which has a much milder winter condition. There are kosher hotels in St. Moritz, Arosa, Engelberg, Grindelwald, and Lugano. They serve both the winter and summer crowds.

The summer crowd in St. Moritz is primarily chassidic. The Vishnitzer Rebbe holds court (*tisch*) in St. Moritz Bad. There is a kosher food section in the Co-Op supermarket. There is a list of kosher breads available in the local (non-Jewish) bakery. You can purchase kosher provisions from the owner of the kosher hotel (Edelweiss).

Classical concerts are performed in the St. Moritz Spa at 10:00 a.m. every day. After Sabbath morning services, many of the Jewish tourists attend these free concerts.

Side Trips

Take the train from St. Moritz to the magnificent glaciers at Morteratsch or Bernina Diavolezza. At this point, take the cable car up to a breathtaking view. Continue on the train along this mountain-pass route to the Italian border-town of Tirano. This trip is about three hours of exciting vistas. You can make train connections to Milan from Tirano. It is about four hours further.

By all means try to take the Glacier Express which runs from the St. Moritz area to Chur, Andermatt, Brig, and Zermatt.

Another exciting train ride is to the Jungfraujoch Glacier. At Interlaken Ost, take the train to Grindelwald. There is a kosher hotel in Grindelwald. Continue from Grindelwald up the steep mountainside by cog-railway to Kleiner Scheidegg. There you will be at the mid-way level. You will see hangliders jumping from the cliffs. At this point, you must again change trains. Now the train will enter into the mountainside. It basically becomes a subway ride through the mountain for about 45 minutes.

But once you get out of the tunnel, you will be freezing. The temperature is about 32 degrees, even in the summer. The Jungfraujoch is about 13,000 feet above see level. You will feel as if you are on top of the world. Only go up the Jungfraujoch on a very clear day.

Note: If you are travelling through Europe on the Eurailpass, the trains from Interlaken Ost to Grindelwald and beyond, towards the Jungfrau, are privately owned. The Eurailpass is not good on these routes. The cost of a round-trip up to the Jungfrau is about $60. If you take the early-bird special (before 9:00 a.m.) you can save about $20. In the summer months, this excursion is extremely popular (especially with the Japanese mountain-climbers). It is highly recommended to leave as early as possible, to avoid the crowds.

Zurich

OLD JEWISH QUARTER

The old Jewish quarter of Zurich was located on the other (east) side of the Limmat River. Judengasse used to be on the site of today's Froschaugasse. There used to be an ancient synagogue on the corner of Froschaugasse and Rindermarkt.

GREAT SYNAGOGUE

Lowenstrasse 10   Tel. 201-16-59

The Great Synagogue of Zurich is located just a few short blocks from the world-renowned Banhofstrasse. It was built in 1884 in the Moorish Revival style. The exterior is quite elegant. The interior, however, is stark. The stained-glass windows portray snow crystals. Next to the synagogue is the kosher grocery and butcher.

CHAGALL WINDOWS

Fraumunster Church at Munsterhof Square

Marc Chagall designed five stained-glass windows of which four depict Old Testament themes . He also designed a circular "Creation of the World" window on the south transcept.

JEWISH COMMUNITY CENTER

Lavaterstrasse 33   Tel. 201-55-83

This building houses the community offices, a Jewish day school, library, disco, cultural center, and a kosher restaurant. There is tight security around this building. You will be buzzed into a glass-enclosed anti-room, asked what your business is, and then buzzed into the security guard's area.

FREIGUTSTRASSE SYNAGOGUE

Freigustrasse 37   Tel. 201-67-46

The majority of Zurich's 7,000 Jews live in the Enge section (#7 or #13 trolley). The Freigutstrasse Synagogue was built on top of a hill around the turn of century. It was designed in the Persian or Assyrian style. The decorations on the walls, stained windows, etc, reflect an Art Deco and De Stijl influence.

KOSHER PROVISIONS

Arosa   Metropole Hotel   *Tel. (081) 311-058*

Basel

Topaz Restaurant   *Leimenstrasse 24   Tel. 22-87-00*

(butcher) *Leimenstrasse 41 Tel. 23-88-35*

Davos

Etania Rest Home   *Tel. (083) 55404*

(grocery) Co-op Supermarket

Engelberg   Hotel Marguerite   *Tel. (041) 94-25-22*

Geneva

Shalom Restaurant   *78 rue du Rhone   Tel. 28-90-93*

(pizza) *50 route de Malagnou*

(bakery-kosher breads available)   *49 rue des Eauvives*

Grindelwald   Silberhorn Hotel *Tel. (036) 53-28-22*

Lausanne

(grocery) *7 avenue Juste Olivier   Tel. (021) 312 12 65*

Lucerne   (butcher)   *Bruchstrasse 26 Tel. 22-25-60*

Lugano Dan Hotel *Via D. Fontana* *Tel.* *(091) 541-061*

St Moritz (Bad)

Edelweiss Hotel *Tel.* *(082) 35533*

(grocery) Co-op Supermarket (Bellevue Hotel)

Zurich

Schalom Restaurant *Lavaterstrasse 33 Tel. 201-1476*

(butcher) *Lowenstrasse 12 Tel. 211-52-10*

(bakery) *Braverstrasse 110 Tel. 242-87-00*

SYNAGOGUES

Arosa Metropole Hotel *Tel.* *(081) 31-10-58*

Baden *Parkstrasse 17 Tel. (056) 26 90 28*

Basel

Leimenstrasse 24 Tel. (061) 23 98 50

Ahornstrasse 14 Tel. (061) 301 48 98

Bern *Kapellenstrasse 2 Tel. (031) 25 49 92*

Biel *Ruchlisstrasse 3 Tel. (032) 23 21 66*

Bremgarten *Antonigasse 53 Tel. (057) 33 37 30*

Davos Etania Rest Home *Tel. (083) 5 54 04*

Engelberg Hotel Marguerite *Tel. (041) 94-25-22*

Fribourg *9 avenue de Rome Tel. (037) 22 16 70*

Geneva

Great Synagogue *place de la Synagogue*

Machsikei Hadass *2 place des Eaux Tel. (022) 47 14 38*

Hekhal Haness

45 route de Malagnou Tel. (022) 736 96 32

Grindelwald Silberhorn Hotel *Tel.* *(036) 53-28-22*

Kreuzlingen *Hafenstrasse 42 Tel. (072) 77 21 96*

La Chaux de Fonds   *rue de Parc 63   Tel. (039) 23 04 77*

Lausanne   *avenue Juste Olivier 1   Tel. (021) 20 66 94*

Luzern *Bruchstrasse 51   Tel. (041) 22 04 00*

Lugano   *11 Via Maderno   Tel. (091) 23 61 34*

Dan Hotel   Via D. Fontana   Tel. (091)54 10 61

Montreux *avenue des Alpes 25   Tel. 61-58-39*

St. Gallen   *Frongartenstrasse 18   Tel. (071) 23 59 23*

St. Moritz (Bad)   Hotel Edelweiss   *Tel. (082) 35533*

Solothurn   *C. Amiet-Straase 4   Tel. (065) 23 11 34*

Vevey *3, Boulevard Plumhof   Tel. (021) 923 53 54*

Winterthur   *Rosenstrasse 5   Tel. (052) 29 81 36*

Yverdon   *26 bis rue Valentin   Tel. (024) 21 18 51*

Zurich

Freigutstrasse 37   Tel. (01) 201 49 98

Erikastrasse 8   Tel. (01) 463 79 20

Lowenstrasse 10   Tel. (01) 201 16 59

Machsikei Hadass *Awandstrasse 59   Tel. (01) 241 37 98*

Minjan Brunau

Mutschellenstrasse 11-15   Tel. (01) 202 51 67

Minjan Belz   *Weststrase 151   Tel. (01) 463 65 98*

Minjan Wollishofen   *Etzelstrasse 6*

Chabad Lubavitch   *Manessestrasse 198   Tel. (01) 201 16 91*

Beth Medrash Chassidei Ger   *Tel. (01) 242 38 99*

MIKVEHS

Arosa   Metropole Hotel   *Tel. (081) 311-058*

Basel   *Tel. (061) 23 29 20   or 301 68 31*

Davos   Etania Rest Home   *Tel. (083) 55404*

Geneva   *54 route de Malagnou   Tel. (022) 736 96 32*

Grindelwald Silberhorn Hotel *Tel. (036) 532-822*

Lucerne *Bruchstrasse 51 Tel. (041) 45 47 50*

Lugano *11 Via Maderno Tel. (091) 23-61-34*

Lausanne *Tel. (021) 29 98 20*

St. Moritz Edelweiss Hotel *Tel. (082) 35533*

Zurich

Freigutstrasse 37 Tel. (01) 201-73-06

Erikastrasse 8 Tel. 463-79-25

RAILROAD TIMETABLE

Zurich to:		
Amsterdam	7:57 - 17:46
Frankfurt	9:57 - 14:17
Geneva	9:03 - 11:58
Milan	8:07 - 12:35
Munich	7:07 - 11:24
Paris	9:57 - 16:16
Rome	8:39 - 19:13
Venice	8:39 - 16:38
Vienna	9:34 - 19:00

Sabbath Candlelighting Timetable

Amsterdam

		Starts	Ends			Starts	Ends
Jan.	4	16:21	17:40	**Jul.**	5	20:15	23:20
	11	16:30	17:49		12	20:15	23:12
	18	16:41	17:58		19	20:05	23:01
	25	16:54	18:09		26	20:00	22:48
Feb.	1	17:06	18:21	**Aug.**	2	19:50	22:33
	8	17:20	18:33		9	19:40	22:18
	15	17:33	18:45		16	19:25	22:01
	22	17:46	18:57		23	19:25	21:44
Mar.	1	18:10	19:10		30	19:05	21:27
	8	18:25	19:22	**Sept.**	6	18:55	21:09
	15	18:35	19:35		13	18:40	20:52
	22	18:50	19:47		20	18:30	20:33
	29	19:00	20:00		28	18:10	20:14
Apr.	5	19:00	21:14	**Oct.**	5	18:10	18:58
	12	19:00	21:27		12	17:50	18:42
	19	19:10	21:41		19	17:17	18:28
	26	19:20	21:55		26	17:02	18:14
May	3	19:30	22:10	**Nov.**	2	16:49	18:02
	10	19:40	22:10		9	16:36	17:51
	17	19:50	22:39		16	16:26	17:41
	24	20:00	22:53		23	16:17	17:34
	31	20:05	23:05		30	16:11	17:29
Jun.	7	20:10	23:15	**Dec.**	7	16:07	17:27
	14	20:15	23:22		14	16:06	17:26
	21	20:20	23:25		21	16:09	17:29
	28	20:20	23:24		28	16:13	17:33

Copenhagen

		Starts	Ends			Starts	Ends
Jan.	4	15:45	16:40	Jul.	5	20:00	23:00
	11	15:45	16:50		12	20:00	22:55
	18	16:00	17:00		19	19:45	22:45
	25	16:15	17:10		26	19:30	22:30
Feb.	1	16:30	17:40	Aug.	2	19:15	22:15
	8	17:00	17:55		9	19:00	22:00
	15	17:00	18:10		16	18:45	21:40
	22	17:10	18:25		23	18:30	21:25
Mar.	1	17:30	18:35		30	18:15	21:05
	8	17:45	18:50	Sept.	6	18:00	20:45
	15	18:00	19:05		13	18:00	20:25
	22	18:00	19:20		20	18:00	20:05
	29	18:15	19:35		28	18:10	19:40
Apr.	5	18:30	19:50	Oct.	5	18:10	18:25
	12	18:45	21:05		12	17:50	18:05
	19	18:45	21:15		19	17:17	17:55
	26	19:00	21:35		26	17:02	17:50
May	3	19:00	21:50	Nov.	2	16:49	17:20
	10	19:15	22:10		9	16:36	17:15
	17	19:30	22:25		16	16:26	16:55
	24	19:45	22:45		23	16:17	16:50
	31	20:00	22:55		30	16:11	16:45
Jun.	7	20:00	23:05	Dec.	7	16:07	16:40
	14	20:00	23:05		14	16:06	16:44
	21	20:00	23:05		21	16:09	16:35
	28	20:00	23:05		28	16:13	16:35

London

		Starts	Ends			Starts	Ends
Jan.	4	15:45	17:03	Jul.	5	20:59	22:31
	11	15:54	17:11		12	20:54	22:24
	18	16:05	17:21		19	20:47	22:14
	25	16:17	17:31		26	20:38	20:02
Feb.	1	16:30	17:43	Aug.	2	20:27	21:48
	8	16:42	17:54		9	20:14	21:33
	15	16:55	18:06		16	20:01	21:17
	22	17:08	18:18		23	19:46	21:00
Mar.	1	17:20	18:30		30	19:31	20:44
	8	17:32	18:42	Sept.	6	19:21	20:34
	15	17:45	18:54		13	19:13	20:24
	22	17:56	19:06		20	19:01	20:14
	29	18:08	19:18		28	18:24	19:34
Apr.	5	19:20	20:31	Oct.	5	18:09	19:34
	12	19:32	20:44		12	17:53	19:03
	19	19:43	20:58		19	17:38	18:48
	26	19:55	21:11		26	17:24	18:35
May	3	20:06	21:25	Nov.	2	16:11	17:23
	10	20:18	21:39		9	15:59	17:12
	17	20:28	21:53		16	15:49	17:04
	24	20:38	22:06		23	15:41	16:57
	31	20:47	22:17		30	15:35	16:52
Jun.	7	20:54	22:26	Dec.	7	15:32	16:49
	14	20:58	22:33		14	15:31	16:49
	21	21:01	22:36		21	15:33	16:52
	28	21:01	22:35		28	15:38	16:56

Nice

		Starts	Ends			Starts	Ends
Jan.	4	16:40	17:52	Jul.	5	20:00	22:03
	11	16:50	17:59		12	20:00	21:57
	18	16:55	18:07		19	20:00	21:50
	25	17:05	18:15		26	20:00	21:42
Feb.	1	17:15	18:24	Aug.	2	20:00	21:30
	8	17:20	18:32		9	20:00	21:20
	15	17:30	18:42		16	20:00	21:07
	22	17:45	18:55		23	20:00	20:56
Mar.	1	17:50	18:59		30	19:30	20:44
	8	18:00	19:07	Sept.	6	19:15	20:30
	15	18:05	19:16		13	19:05	10:16
	22	18:15	19:24		20	19:00	20:03
	29	18:20	19:33		28	17:40	18:49
Apr.	5	19:30	20:41	Oct.	5	17:25	18:38
	12	19:40	20:52		12	17:15	18:26
	19	20:00	21:01		19	17:05	18:15
	26	20:00	21:10		26	16:55	18:06
May	3	20:00	21:19	Nov.	2	16:53	18:04
	10	20:00	21:27		9	16:45	17:55
	17	20:00	21:37		16	16:40	17:48
	24	20:00	21:44		23	16:35	17:44
	31	20:00	21:52		30	16:30	17:42
Jun.	7	20:00	21:58	Dec.	7	16:30	17:40
	14	20:00	22:03		14	16:30	17:40
	21	20:00	22:06		21	16:30	17:43
	28	20:00	22:07		28	16:35	17:47

Paris

		Starts	Ends			Starts	Ends
Jan.	4	16:48	18:02	Jul.	5	21:36	23:00
	11	16:57	18:10		12	21:32	22:55
	18	17:07	18:19		19	21:26	22:46
	25	17:17	18:28		26	21:18	22:36
Feb.	1	17:29	18:38	Aug.	2	21:08	22:24
	8	17:40	18:49		9	20:57	22:11
	15	17:52	19:00		16	20:45	21:57
	22	18:03	19:10		23	20:18	21:27
Mar.	1	18:14	19:21		30	20:03	21:11
	8	18:25	19:32	Sept.	6	19:49	20:56
	15	18:36	19:43		13	19:35	20:48
	22	18:47	19:54		20	18:26	19:37
	29	18:57	20:05		28	18:16	19:25
Apr.	5	20:08	21:16	Oct.	5	18:02	19:08
	12	20:18	21:27		12	17:47	18:54
	19	20:28	21:39		19	17:34	18:41
	26	20:39	21:51		26	17:21	18:29
May	3	20:49	22:03	Nov.	2	17:09	18:18
	10	20:59	22:15		9	16:59	18:08
	17	21:08	22:27		16	16:50	18:00
	24	21:17	22:38		23	16:43	17:54
	31	21:25	22:47		30	16:38	17:50
Jun.	7	21:31	22:55	Dec.	7	16:35	17:49
	14	21:36	23:01		14	16:35	17:49
	21	21:38	23:04		21	16:37	17:51
	28	21:38	23:04		28	16:42	17:56

Rome

		Starts	Ends			Starts	Ends
Jan.	4	16:32	17:38	Jul.	5	20:28	21:40
	11	16:39	17:45		12	20:25	21:36
	18	16:47	17:52		19	20:21	21:30
	25	16:56	18:00		26	20:15	21:23
Feb.	1	17:05	18:08	Aug.	2	20:08	21:14
	8	17:14	18:17		9	19:59	21:05
	15	17:23	18:25		16	19:49	20:54
	22	17:32	18:33		23	19:39	20:42
Mar.	1	17:40	18:41		30	19:27	20:30
	8	17:48	18:50	Sept.	6	19:16	20:18
	15	17:56	18:58		13	19:03	20:05
	22	18:04	19:06		20	18:50	19:52
	29	18:12	19:14		28	18:37	19:38
Apr.	5	19:20	20:22	Oct.	5	17:25	18:26
	12	19:28	20:30		12	17:13	18:15
	19	19:35	20:39		19	17:02	18:04
	26	19:43	20:48		26	16:52	17:54
May	3	19:51	20:57	Nov.	2	16:43	17:46
	10	19:58	21:05		9	16:35	17:38
	17	20:05	21:14		16	16:28	17:33
	24	20:12	21:21		23	16:23	17:28
	31	20:18	21:18		30	16:20	17:26
Jun.	7	20:23	21:34	Dec.	7	16:19	17:25
	14	20:27	21:38		14	16:20	17:26
	21	20:29	21:41		21	16:22	17:29
	28	20:28	21:40		28	16:26	17:33

Zurich		Starts	Ends			Starts	Ends
Jan.	4	16:29	17:41	Jul.	5	21:05	22:26
	11	16:37	17:48		12	21:01	22:21
	18	16:47	17:57		19	20:56	22:13
	25	16:57	18:06		26	20:48	22:04
Feb.	1	17:08	18:16	Aug.	2	20:39	21:52
	8	17:19	18:26		9	20:28	21:40
	15	17:29	18:36		16	20:17	21:27
	22	17:40	18:46		23	20:04	21:13
Mar.	1	17:51	18:56		30	19:51	20:58
	8	18:01	19:07	Sept.	6	19:37	20:43
	15	18:11	19:17		13	19:23	20:29
	22	18:21	19:27		20	19:05	20:15
	29	18:31	19:37	Sept.	28	18:52	19:57
Apr.	5	19:41	20:48	Oct.	5	17:38	18:43
	12	19:51	20:59		12	17:24	18:29
	19	20:01	21:10		19	17:11	18:17
	26	20:10	21:21		26	16:59	18:05
May	3	20:20	21:32	Nov.	2	16:47	17:55
	10	20:29	21:43		9	16:38	17:46
	17	20:38	21:54		16	16:29	17:38
	24	20:47	22:04		23	16:23	17:33
	31	20:54	22:13		30	16:18	17:29
Jun.	7	21:00	22:21	Dec.	7	16:16	17:27
	14	21:04	22:26		14	16:16	17:28
	21	21:07	22:29		21	16:18	17:30
	28	21:07	22:29		28	16:23	17:35

Bibliography

Aguilar, M. & Robertson, I. *Jewish Spain-A Guide*

Altalena Editores, Madrid, 1984

Altshuler, D. *The Precious Legacy*

Summit Books, New York, 1983

Barnett, R.D. & Levy, A. *The Bevis Marks Synagogue*

University Press, Oxford, 1975

Bocher, O. *Der Alter Judenfriedhof zu Worms*

Rheinische Kunststatten, Neuss, 1984

Cohen, S.R. *Scandinavia's Jewish Communities*

The American Scandinavian Review, Summer, 1968

de Breffny, B. *The Synagogue*

Macmillan Publishing Co. Inc., New York, 1978

Diamond, A.S. *The Building of a Synagogue*

West London Synagogue

Encyclopedia Judaica   Keter Publishing, Jerusalem, 1972

Flender, H. *Rescue in Denmark*

Simon and Schuster, New York, 1963

Frank, B. G. *France for the Jewish Traveler*

Air France, French Government Tourist Office, French Press and Information Services, and French National   Railroads, 1982

Gans, M. H. M.

History of Dutch Jewry from the Renaissance to 1940

Bosch & Keuning, Baarn, Netherlands, 1977

Girard, P. Orland-Hajdenberg, E. Douvette,D.

Guide du Judaisme Français   Judeomedias, Paris, 1987

Grand, S. & Grand, T.

Exploring the Jewish Heritage in Spain   Spanish National
Tourist Office, Spain, 1980

Jarrassé,D. *L'Age d'Or des Synagogues.*

Paris. Editions

Jewish Rome

Cultural Movement of Students, Emanuel Pacifici, Jewish
Community of Rome, Rabbinical Office of Rome, Centre for
Jewish Culture, Rabbi Prof. Toaff, Prof. Saban, Armando
Tagliacozzo, Rome,1983

Kahn, L. *Geschichte der Synagogen in Basel*

Israelitische Gemeinde Basel, 1968

Krinsky, C. H. *Synagogues of Europe*

MIT Press, Cambridge, Mass., 1985

Levenson, G. *Jewish Life in Scandinavia*

SAS Scandinavian Airlines, 1973

Levi, L. *Jewish Chronometry*

Ministry of Religious Affairs, Jerusalem, 1983

Lightman, S. *The Jewish Travel Guide*

Jewish Chronicle, London, 1989

Maier, M. *The Jewish Cemetery of Worms,* 1984

Mendleson, C. *The Jewish Museum Guide*

Woburn House, London

Metzger, T. & M. *Jewish Life in the Middle Ages*

Chartwell Books, New Jersey, 1982

Postal, B. & Abramson, S.H.

Traveler's Guide to Jewish Landmarks of Europe

Fleet Press Corp., New York, 1979

Sacerdoti, A. *Guide to Jewish Italy*
Israelowitz Publishing, New York, 1989

Servi, S. *The Synagogue of Florence*
Florence Jewish Community, Florence, 1982

Storti, E. *Jews and Synagogues of Venice, Florence, Rome, and Livorno* Venice, 1973

Stoutenbeek, J. & Vigeveno, P. *Guide to Jewish Amsterdam*
Jewish Historical Society - De Haan, Amsterdam, 1985

Synagogues in 19th Century Germany
Catalogue, Beth Hatefutsoth, The Nahum Goldmann Museum of the Jewish Diaspora, Tel Aviv, 1982

Tigay, M. *The Jewish Traveler*
Doubleday & Company, New York, 1987

Wigoder, G. *Jewish Art and Civilization*
Chartwell Books, New Jersey, 1972

Wischnitzer, R. *The Architecture of European Synagogues*
The Jewish Publication Society of America, Philadelphia, 1963

Vega, L. A. *The Beth Haim of Ouderkerk aan de Amstel*
Van Gorcum & Co, B.V., Assen, Netherlands, 1979

Yahil, L. *The Rescue of Danish Jewry*
Jewish Publication Society, Philadelphia, 1969

Catalog

SYNAGOGUES of the UNITED STATES

by Oscar Israelowitz $29.95

GUIDE to JEWISH EUROPE - 8th Edition

by Oscar Israelowitz $11.95

GUIDE to JEWISH ITALY

by Annie Sacerdoti $12.95

GUIDE to JEWISH NEW YORK CITY

by Oscar Israelowitz $9.95

EAT YOUR WAY through AMERICA & CANADA

by Oscar Israelowitz $5.95

LOWER EAST SIDE GUIDE

by Oscar Israelowitz $6.95

ELLIS ISLAND GUIDE

by Oscar Israelowitz $7.95

CANADA JEWISH TRAVEL GUIDE

by Oscar Israelowitz $9.95

UNITED STATES JEWISH TRAVEL GUIDE

by Oscar Israelowitz $14.95

SO THIS WAS BROOKLYN - Early Views

by Israelowitz & Merlis $19.95

EARLY VIEWS of BOROUGH PARK

by Oscar Israelowitz $4.95

FLATBUSH GUIDE

by Oscar Israelowitz $4.95

CATSKILLS GUIDE

by Oscar Israelowitz $4.95

GUIDE to JEWISH CANADA & U.S.A. (Northeast)

by Oscar Israelowitz $11.95

GUIDE to JEWISH U.S.A. (South-Vol. II)

by Oscar Israelowitz $9.95

GUIDE to the JEWISH WEST

by Oscar Israelowitz $11.95

NEW YORK CITY SUBWAY GUIDE

by Oscar Israelowitz $6.95

NOTE: ADD $2.00 PER TITLE - SHIPPING CHARGE.

ENCYCLOPEDIA JUDAICA (17 volumes)................$700.00

   YEARBOOKS (1973-82), (1983-85), (1986-87), (1988-89)

   1990-91 YEARBOOK (Each) $75.00

ALCALAY DICTIONARY (3 vol.)............................$90.00

MY DICTIONARY (Childrens)....................................$15.00

MY LITTLE DICTIONARY...$8.00

CHRONICLES (New - in one volume).....................$30.00

SKYLINE (Aerial Views of Israel).............................$40.00

ISRAEL ROOTS & ROUTES...$40.00

PILLAR OF FIRE...$75.00

THE WESTERN WALL...$20.00

ISRAEL, NEVER A DULL MOMENT...........................$25.00

HEBREW FOR ENGLISH SPEAKERS

                        (3 cassettes & book)...$25.00

ISRAEL ON A BUDGET...$20.00

CHRONOLOGY IN THE BIBLE (Shulman)................$25.00

THE HALACHA (E. Urbach)......................................$30.00

LISBON BIBLE (1482 Facsimile)...............................$90.00

COPENHAGEN HAGGADAH (1739 Facsimile)...........$25.00

STUDIES IN THE BIBLE (6 vol.) N. Leibowitz..........$95.00

ADD $2.00 PER TITLE - SHIPPING CHARGE.

Israelowitz Publishing

P.O.Box 228   Brooklyn, New York 11229   Tel. (718) 951-7072

ENCYCLOPEDIA TO THE HOLOCAUST (4 vol.).....$300.00

JEWISH HOLIDAYS (Renberg)..................................$22.95

ENCYCLOPEDIA OF THE JEWISH RELIGION.........$39.95

OFF THE BEATEN TRACK IN ISRAEL (Devir)..........$24.95

KOSHER ITALIAN GOURMET (Aharoni).................$22.95

THE PASSOVER GOURMET (Rousso)......................$22.95

JEWISH HOLIDAY CAKES (Shaulov)........................$22.95

ADD $2.00 PER TITLE - SHIPPING CHARGE.

Israelowitz Publishing

P.O.Box 228 Brooklyn, New York 11229 Tel. (718) 951-7072

BIOGRAPHY

Oscar Israelowitz was born in Brussels, Belgium. He is an architectural consultant by profession. Some of his projects include the Synagogue and Holocaust Center of the Bobover chassidim and the Yeshiva Rabbi Chaim Berlin (both in Brooklyn, NY). He has also designed homes and villas for clients in the United States, Haiti and Israel.

Mr. Israelowitz is also a professional photographer. His works have been on exhibit in the Whitney Museum of American Art, Brooklyn Museum, Brooklyn Historical Society and Yeshiva University Museum. One of his exhibits is on permanent display in the New York Transit Museum.

Oscar Israelowitz has appeared on several television and radio programs including the *Joe Franklin Show*, NBC's *First Estate - Religion in Review,* and Ruth Jacob's *Jewish Home Show.*

In more recent years. Mr. Israelowitz has been conducting tours of Ellis Island, the Lower East Side, Jewish Baltimore & Washington, D.C., and the Jewish Caribbean. These tours have been written-up in *New York Magazine,* the *Washington Post,* the *Los Angeles Times* and the *Chicago Tribune.*

INDEX

TOURS OF JEWISH NEW YORK CITY...

* Lower East Side
* Colonial Jewish New York
* Ellis Island
* Chassidic Neighborhoods of Brooklyn
* Boat Tour of Jewish New York

Israelowitz Tours

P.O.Box 228   Brooklyn, New York 11229

Tel. (718) 951-7072

Tours

LOWER EAST SIDE TOUR

Visit the "old neighborhood" with stops at the old Forward Building, the last yeshiva, a landmark synagogue, Orchard Street and, of course, Guss' Pickles.

ELLIS ISLAND TOUR

This tour starts as a walking tour of the Colonial Jewish settlement of New Amsterdam. See the Jewish Plymouth Rock, Holocaust Museum site and Castle Garden. This is followed by a ferry ride to Ellis Island and an additional tour of the Immigration Museum.

CHASSIDIC NEIGHBORHOODS OF BROOKLYN

Visit Williamsburg, Boro Park and Crown Heights. See the great synagogues, eat in an old fashion kosher restaurant, and visits to a mikveh and/or matzoh bakery.

BOAT TOUR OF JEWISH NEW YORK

Enjoy a delightful three-hour tour of the Jewish sites around New York harbor. Sites include: Statue of Liberty, Ellis Island Immigration Museum, Jewish "Plymouth Rock," the Lower East Side, Williamsburg, the United Nations, Mt. Sinai Hospital, Yeshiva University, Washington Heights and the Upper West Side.

Israelowitz Tours

P.O.Box 228 Brooklyn, NY 11229   Tel. (718) 951-7072

JEWISH HUDSON VALLEY

Tour includes stops at the West Point Jewish Chapel, a stone house built by a Sephardic Jew during Colonial times, wine-tasting in a kosher winery and a visit to a 200-year-old grist mill where flour is ground to make Passover matzohs.

JEWISH NEW ENGLAND

Visit the Touro Synagogue, Boston historic districts, the American Jewish Historical Society and Museum at Brandeis, the great university campuses and much more.

JEWISH FARMERS OF NEW JERSEY

Visit the remaining Jewish poultry farmers of southern New Jersey. Stops include a "shtetl" style synagogue, a rabbinical academy and a chicken farm. You can purchase the freshest eggs in town - directly from the farmer.

JEWISH WASHINGTON & BALTIMORE

Tour historic Baltimore with stops at the historic Lloyd Street Synagogue and Museum, the Inner Harbor and the National Aquarium. The tour continues to the nation's Capitol with visits to the great museums and monuments plus a visit to the new United States Holocaust Memorial Museum and the headquarters of B'nai B'rith International and its newly-restored Klutznick Museum.

JEWISH PHILADELPHIA

Visit the oldest Sephardic congregation in the city, the Liberty Bell, the National Museum of American Jewish History and a synagogue designed by Frank Lloyd Wright.

Note: All tour itineraries subject to change.

JEWISH CARIBBEAN

Grand Caribbean Cruise with stops at some of the oldest Jewish communities in the Western Hemisphere. Islands included in tour: Curaçao, St. Thomas, Barbados, ⁵ Eustatius, St. Martin and Guadeloupe.

JEWISH MONTREAL

Visit this charming European-style city with its old Jewish "East Side," great art museums, the world's quietest and loveliest subway system, Jewish art galleries and quaint cafes.

JEWISH TORONTO

Tour Toronto's old Jewish neighborhoods and then journey to the present-day sections which contain wonderful kosher restaurants, theatres and cafes, world-class Jewish museums and galleries and much more. Tour stops at Niagara Falls on the way.

JEWISH LONDON, PARIS, AMSTERDAM

The grand tour of the great Jewish centers of London includes visits to the East End and Golders Green, the Bevis Marks Synagogue, the Jewish Museum and the newly-designed Canary Wharf - Docklands Project. We take the hovercraft or the new English Channel Tunnel, the "Chunnel," to France.

The Paris tour includes visits to the old Jewish centers along rue des Rosiers and rue Montmartre with their great kosher restaurants and cafes, the Pompidou Centre, the Eifel Tower, Jewish museums and galleries, and the great Rothschild Synagogue.

The Amsterdam tour includes visits to the Great Portuguese Synagogue, the new Jewish Historical Museum, Rembrandt' House, the old Jewish neighborhood, the Rijksmuseum and Ann Frank's House.

NOTES

NOTES

NOTES

NOTAS